A LIFE UNSTARTED

A chance at a new life, a past that refuses to stay buried, and a dangerous encounter that threatens it all.

ISABELLA WILES

Emily,

Just a little teaser to give you a flavour of what's to come,

Izzy

Aurora Independent Publishing

The Three Great Loves of Victoria Turnbull

PREQUEL NOVELLA

A LIFE UNSTARTED

The Turk

A nail biting coming-of-age story about the power of friendship, and searching for love in all the wrong places.

ISABELLA WILES

Other books by Isabella Wiles

THE THREE GREAT LOVES OF
VICTORIA TURNBULL SERIES

A Life Unstarted - A novella (Prequel)

A Flame Unburned - The Kiwi (Book 1)

A Promise Unmade - The Geordie (Book 2)

A Star Unborn - The Celt (Book 3)

Connect with Isabella at:
www.isabellawiles.com

Join Isabella's online book club:
facebook.com/groups/IzzysReadingBees

facebook.com/IsabellaWiles
instagram.com/isabellawiles_author

For all my fabulous readers.
This bonus novella is especially for you.
Thank you for all your continued
love and support.

And for Tunney, who lived it with me.

Contents

Part One

Chapter 1

VICTORIA

Wiltshire, England, May 1992

Switching off the engine, I glance at my watch. Shit!

Still, I'm only fifteen minutes late. Taking a sip from the can of cola balanced in my central console, the sweet nectar fizzes on my tongue before sliding down my gullet and joining forces with the butterflies in my tummy. I was already excited when I left home nine hours ago—my only focus the future I was travelling towards. The tarmac stretching endlessly in front of me, pulling me forward with little thought to what I was leaving behind—but now that I'm here, and what was once familiar is beyond the reach of my outstretched fingers—my butterflies of excitement have morphed into ones of trepidation.

What if this is a mistake? I glance in my rear-view mirror. No, this was my choice, and it's what I want.

Rapping my fingers against the steering wheel, I look beyond the nose of my car bonnet. The sun is sinking, throwing its last rays of burnt orange and blood red across the cloudless sky.

Where the hell is he?

A new job. A new home. Moving to the opposite end of the country, where I know no-one other than my new-ish boyfriend who I'm about to move in with—my first ever cohabiting relationship. I'm definitely taking a gigantic leap into a new adventure. A new life. A new start, at last.

When I called him two hours ago from the payphone at the motorway services, we calculated the time I'd arrive at our meeting point. So why is he not here? He must have been held up. Or maybe he's doing some last-minute chores, making sure the house is clean and tidy for my arrival. I imagine him cooking up an aromatic curry for supper, or stopping at the garage to pick up a bunch of flowers, wanting to make my transition down here a bit easier. He knows it's an enormous step I'm taking. A real leap of faith.

Living at opposite ends of the country, in the five months Steve and I have been dating I initially either flew down to Bristol, or travelled by train to spend the weekend with him. But because it's so far, the travel time ate into most of the weekend, so more recently we've met somewhere in the middle, staying in B&Bs for a snatched Saturday night away. Therefore, worried I'd get lost in the twisting lanes of deepest-darkest Wiltshire, it had been his idea to meet in a lay-by off the motorway and drive the last fifteen miles in convoy.

My stomach grumbles and I stifle a sickly burp. I scan around the car, but I've nothing left to eat. The crisps and Mars Bars I'd brought with me are long gone. And in my eagerness to get here, I didn't think about picking up food at the services.

I suck in a deep breath and shake my wrists, trying to knock out my nerves. A few weeks ago, when I decided to relocate my life to take our relationship to the next level, it seemed like the right thing to do. In fact, the only thing to do. But sitting in a deserted lay-by, not knowing where he is, or what might have happened to him – I feel very alone. Vulnerable and abandoned.

I crane my neck looking for a glimpse of his car coming into view, but all I see are rolling green hills sprawling out in every direction, punctuated by the odd church spire stabbing the sky.

I bite my lip when I think back to how I'd allowed my mind to run away with me on the long drive down here. Images of us, in a year or two, moving out of his rental and buying our first home together. Decorating it in soft hues of cream and blue – just like the pictures I've seen in all those lifestyle magazines. Or the two of us on holiday, chinking glasses as we curl up on our veranda watching the sun slip below the horizon in some far-flung exotic location. I place my palms over my flushed cheeks as I recall another vision; the ultimate dream. Me, a vision in white. Him, smartly turned out in a traditional morning suit. Us, standing together at the front of my packed village church back in the north-east of England. The ladies' huge hats and wide shoulder pads bumping up against each other as everyone cranes their necks to get the best view of us at the altar. Isn't that what everyone wants? The dream? The happily ever after fairy-tale ending?

I'm jolted back to reality, my hand flying to my heart as someone taps a knuckle on my car window. A pair of stern eyes, set within a weather-worn face, peer inside the glass. The word 'police' screams at me from the man's black ribbed V-neck jumper as he indicates for me to wind down my window.

"Everything all right, miss?" His eyes scan the inside of my car.

"Err, yes. I'm fine."

He pauses, as if deciding whether he should comment on what he sees. My illegally overloaded car and obscured rear-view mirror. "What's your name?" he asks.

"Victoria Turnbull."

"Have you broken down, or are you not feeling well?"

"No officer. I'm waiting for my boyfriend." I sit on my hands so he can't see them shaking. I've never come this close to an officer of the law before, never mind had one talk to me.

"Well, if everything's okay, I'm going to need you to move on. This lay-by is for emergency vehicles only and it's an offence to park here."

"Oh, I'm so sorry. I had no idea. Of course. I'll move now." I fumble with my key in the ignition.

Giving him a terse smile, I wind my window back up and check my watch again. Six-thirty-five. Damn you Steve, where the hell are you?

I could try to find a phone box. Leave him a message on his

answerphone at home. But I don't have any more change on me. I'd have to find a shop first, use a five-pound note and buy something cheap, then hunt down a payphone. Or maybe I could try to find another safe place to park nearby. Or maybe I should just chance it. See if I can navigate my way to his house. Hopefully he'll be there, waiting for me having lost track of time.

The police officer steps back and twirls his index finger, ushering me to get going.

Turning the key in the ignition and dropping the car into gear, I give the police officer a cursory wave and make to pull out, but the car lurches to a halt. I yank on the handbrake and return the gear stick to neutral. Starting the car a second time, I slowly release the clutch, but my foot slips and I stall again. My hands shaking on the steering wheel, I bite my lip and use every ounce of strength to hold in my tears.

The police officer walks up to the window a second time and smiles warmly.

I wind down the glass and blink hard in quick succession.

"Take a deep breath," he says in a warm paternal voice. "You're not in any trouble." He presses his lips into another smile.

"At least not yet, anyway." I make to laugh, but it comes out more like a snort. Like a dog blowing out a puff of air from its nose.

"I'll hold the traffic for you. Just take your time and pull out slowly," he says in a kind voice. "You'll be absolutely fine."

I do as he says and start the engine again. Taking my time I check my mirrors and edge forward onto the main road. Glancing in my rear-view mirror, the uniformed officer has already turned on his heel, one hand on the walk-talkie clipped to his body vest as he tilts his head towards it. Presumably giving information to or receiving information from his control centre.

If only I had a control centre to tell me if I'm travelling down the right road, and tell me what to do if I'm not. I press the accelerator and the car responds.

Oh well, I've come this far. I suppose I just have to keep going.

Chapter 2

My little Renault 5 twists and turns down unfamiliar roads, and I suppress the panic tightening in my gut. Nothing looks familiar, so I try to head in the general direction of Steve's village, on the outskirts of Chippenham, but this part of England is littered with unmarked single-track roads, and it's easy to get lost.

Twenty minutes later, I happen across a familiar crossroads, marked by an old-style fingerpost sign. Its wooden arms painted white and inscribed with the names of four villages shoot off in perpendicular directions. The prickles on the back of my neck confirm that I'm almost there, and the Happy Ever After I've always dreamed of is within touching distance. I imagine what it will be like to arrive at Steve's cottage and run into his waiting arms.

'You made it,' he'll say, a proud smile on his face as he envelops me in a hug. *'I must have got my timings muddled up and by the time I got there I knew I'd missed you. So I pelted back home. I figured you'd call if you got lost.'*

Then he'll pick me up and twirl me around before planting an inviting kiss on my welcoming lips.

'Get yourself inside. The kettle's just boiled and I suspect you'll want a cuppa after that long drive.'

'But what about all my stuff?'

'Don't worry. I'll sort it,' he'll say, sending me into the house with a gentle slap on my bum.

I turn onto a road I recognise and arch my back in my seat, attempting to stretch away the stiffness in my spine. Not long now.

I spy a village Co-op and pull over. Running inside, I grab a bottle of champagne. I can't really afford luxuries on my measly wage, but this is a moment worth celebrating. Plus, if he's bought me flowers, I'll feel bad if I rock up empty-handed.

"Special occasion?" the shop assistant asks.

"Kind of." I dip my head. "I'm new to the area. I'm moving in with my boyfriend and I start a new job on Monday."

"Well, congratulations, and I don't wish to be rude, but could I see some ID please?"

"Of course." I open my purse and pull out my Student Railcard. I may be twenty-one, and well past the legal drinking age, but I'm used to being ID'd, unless I'm out with Steve. Perhaps the ten-year age gap makes me appear more mature when I'm on his arm.

"Here you go, love." The shop assistant passes me the bottle. "And welcome to Wiltshire. It's a lovely part of the world. I've lived here all my life and wouldn't want to move anywhere else."

"Thank you."

"As you're going to be living locally, I wonder if I could interest you in a couple of raffle tickets for the children's hospice. There are some lovely prizes for the winner, and of course all the money raised is going to a great cause." She points to the shelf behind her where a couple of cellophane-wrapped hampers, their lids open, are overflowing with pots of chutneys, home-made jams, and bottles of wine.

"Of course. Here, take my change." I drop the coins into her palm and she passes me a couple of strips of raffle tickets, writing my name and Steve's telephone number in her book of stubs.

"On behalf of the children, thank you. We'll be in touch if you win."

I smile and head out of the shop.

A few minutes later, with my knees trembling, I turn into Steve's lane, expecting to see his car parked up outside his two-bed farm-worker's cottage, the middle terrace in a row of three, but the space outside his house remains empty. Shit! If he's not here, I have no way of getting inside. He's not yet given me a key.

Yanking on the handbrake, I think through my options. I could try to retrace my steps. See if I can find him, assuming he's still out looking for me. But what if we miss each other – again? Maybe I should wait. He has to come back at some point, if only to check his answerphone messages.

As forty-five neon green digits tick by on the car dashboard, the vice-like grip in my gut intensifies. Earlier, when I left my childhood home and joined the A1 trunk road at the start of my journey south, I felt strong and brave. My adventure just beginning. Now, as night falls and the light fades, the surrounding countryside morphs into a very different landscape. Dark lanes without street lights turn the welcoming green hills of earlier into vast plains devoid of life. Even the trees seem possessed, the wind rattling through their branches like the cackle of mythical witches laughing at me and my naiveté. I no longer feel brave and adventurous; I feel small and vulnerable – and very, very lost.

I should have waited by the motorway. Found another spot near the lay-by. Steve must be worried sick by now. Believing me to be smashed up on the motorway somewhere. Then another thought hits me like a bullet through my solar plexus: What if he's the one who's had an accident?

I wipe away the single tear that rolls down my cheek.

Maybe I should go to the police. But I have no idea where the nearest station is. Then, before I've had the chance to organise my thoughts any further, a pair of headlights turn into the lane.

I jump out of my car and run towards the Volvo estate as Steve's car trundles its way through the pot holes of the dirt track. He parks up, gets out, and without waiting I leap into his arms, wrapping my legs around his waist.

"Oh, Steve. You have no idea how pleased I am to see you," I gush, smothering his features with quick, fleeting kisses.

"Where the hell have you been? You were supposed to wait for me," he barks. One by one he peels my arms away from his neck and pushes my legs back down onto the ground.

"I did! But you weren't there. And then a policeman came. I didn't know what to do, so I thought I'd try to remember the way to your house – well…" I dip my head, "I mean, to our home. I thought I'd surprise you."

A shiver ripples across my skin as I think of what I've had to sacrifice to make this move. The memory of my mother and step-father's cold stony faces when I told them of my plans to accept a new job and move in with Steve. I had hoped they'd be excited for me, give me their blessing and wish me well, but they took my decision as a personal rejection. I'm not sure if it was the decision to move so far away that caused their grief, or that I'd chosen a life with my relatively new boyfriend over them. Either way, in the eight weeks since they've not held back in their disapproval. I've endured multiple meals around their dining table in stony silence, the sound of our cutlery scraping across our plates the only dialogue between us. Any attempt at light-hearted conversation met with clipped, one-word responses, which only sped up my eagerness to leave.

'If you could just leave your house key on the side before you go.' My mother's parting shot from earlier today. Her words still as sharp as a bee sting.

Nope, there's no going back now, even if I wanted to.

I reach up and touch Steve's face. "Please don't be grumpy. I'm here now. All safe and sound. Aren't you proud of me?" He looks at me, his eyebrows knitted together. "…I drove myself all the way here *and* found my way to your front door."

"Yeah, well. I waited for over an hour. I thought something had happened to you. Are you sure you had the right lay-by? I was worried sick."

"Yes, Junction Eighteen. Like we agreed."

He rolls his eyes. "No, Victoria. I said Junction Seventeen. That's you all over. Breezing through life, not listening. Not taking caring. When are you ever going to learn?"

His words slap me around the face as if his hand had connected with my cheek. I *know* he said Junction Eighteen, I wrote it down, so either he's the one who didn't listen, or he's lying to cover up his mistake, but I don't want to fight on our first night together, so I swallow down my protestations and say nothing.

"Well, you're here now," he continues. "I expect you'll want to get your stuff inside before it gets much darker." He storms off and unlocks the house, leaving me standing, deflated, in the middle of the lane.

Wiping my eyes with the heel of my hands and ignoring the painful lump in the back of my throat, I lift a box out of the boot. Stumbling under its weight, I follow in Steve's wake, shrinking further and further into my skin.

What have I done?

Maybe the champagne will cheer him up?

Chapter 3

Dumping the box on the floor just inside the front door, I look around. My jaw drops. A discarded pizza box and an overflowing ashtray litter the coffee table, and the hearth is dirty with black ash. Every surface is covered with piles of clothes, presumably waiting to be washed. The room looks like the aftermath of a visit from The Cat in the Hat.

A shiver ripples across my skin.

Steve plonks himself in his armchair, one foot resting across the opposite knee, his nose buried in a magazine, oblivious to the mess.

Shuffling my way past the carnage, I walk through the doorway that leads to the kitchen and the stone in the pit of my stomach sinks further still. All the worktops are strewn with used mugs, their insides stained with tannins or slops of sour tea, while the sink is stacked precariously high with unwashed dishes. Rubbish spills out of the bin onto the dirt-smeared floor. How can anyone live like this?

I close then reopen my eyes but nope, I'm not dreaming. Trudging upstairs I suck in another deep breath and push open the bedroom door with my foot. Gazing around the room, I see it as if for the first time, though I've been here before, and the reality of the corner I've backed myself into hits me like the icy blast that comes through the yellowing net curtains. I open Steve's only wardrobe, hoping for at least one sign that he has made some tiny effort for my arrival, but it's stuffed full. There's no space for my clothes. No space for me.

Surveying the rest of the room, I blink back my tears. The duvet lies unmade, cast in a crumpled heap in the middle of the naked mattress.

"That's it," I hiss through gritted teeth, my hands balling into fists.

Stomping back downstairs, I yank the copy of *Farmer's Weekly* out of Steve's hands. "You couldn't even be bothered to make the bed? You might think it's okay to sleep on a bare mattress, but I have standards."

"I haven't had time. I've been slammed at work all week. Plus, now you're here, I thought you'd do it." He grabs the magazine back, shakes it into shape and continues reading. "I suspect you'll want to get supper started as well. Before it gets too late."

My eyes out on stalks, my jaw falls open again as I'm rendered speechless. As if on auto-pilot, I turn back towards the kitchen, my fairy tale shattered.

This is not the Steve I know. The man who, over the past five months, has cherished me and spoiled me every chance he's got. Sending me flowers to my parents' home the Monday after our weekend get-togethers. His love notes telling me how much he was missing me and how he couldn't wait to see me again.

I still have all those notes. I would sleep with them under my pillow and dream of a time when we wouldn't have to say goodbye on a Sunday afternoon before travelling back to opposite ends of the country.

'If I could pluck the moon from the sky and give it to you, I would,' he'd said, pointing up into the night sky a few months back as we'd strolled back towards our B&B.

How lucky am I? I'd thought. *I've finally found a man who appreciates me.*

My first serious relationship had been with another man ten years my senior, and despite my inexperience, I worshipped him. When all my friends were hanging around the park or going to the local cinema with their teenage boyfriends, I was being treated to fancy dinners and nights out in classy nightclubs. He made me feel much more sophisticated than my nineteen years. I was still a virgin when we met and had hoped he would be the one to lead me across that sacred threshold. Despite my inexperience, I felt like his world orbited around mine – until one day he dropped a bombshell.

'I'm so sorry, Victoria, there's something I need to tell you,' he'd said, clutching my wandering hands and pulling back from a hot, passionate kiss on the night we'd planned to go all the way. How could he smother me with his passion if he insisted on keeping his damn pants on?

'Oh,' I'd half-laughed. *'That sounds ominous.'*

'I won't be making love to you tonight.' He'd stroked my hair as I'd lain on top of him, still in my underwear, he still in his. *'You see, I'm not allowed to.'*

'Not allowed to?'

'Not until I've finished the antibiotics and the infection's cleared up.'

And just like that, he shattered my dreams and broke my trust. By catching an STI, he had to own up to having cheated.

On principle, I ended it immediately. Storming out in a flood of snot-filled tears, even though a part of me wanted to let his indiscretion go. He was a grown man, after all. At ten years my senior, if I wasn't sleeping with him, was it unreasonable for him to be getting his needs met elsewhere? Is a one-night stand ever forgivable?

The first six months of dating him had been absolute bliss, and I've often wondered what would have happened if I hadn't made such a snap decision and been so determined to stand by my principles. The dint to my self-esteem was earth shattering.

After Mr STI, I was desperate to replace the void he'd left behind. I felt empty inside and was constantly searching for 'the one' who would want me.

I eventually lost my virginity at the end of a summer romance, rolling around the sand dunes of the Northumberland coast with a guy who was funny, good-looking and even though we only ever did it the once – as it turns out – a very caring lover. I adored him and wanted to keep dating, but I liked him more than he liked me and, despite my best efforts, he stopped returning my calls when college resumed in the autumn.

There was one time at college when I thought someone was genuinely interested in me. How wrong could I have been? He turned out to be someone else who abused my trust–in the most horrific way. But I can't dwell on what happened. I've forced myself to block it out.

Steve and I met eighteen months later, when my confidence and self-esteem were at an all-time low. I was visiting an old school friend who was studying at Leeds University, and he was doing the same, so although our social circles didn't overlap, he made his move while we were waiting to order drinks at the Union Bar.

He's unlike any of my previous boyfriends. His green chords and plaid shirts give him a look of Farmer Giles, which befits his career as an Agricultural Feed Sales Manager. Tall, with a mop of curly brown hair that sits above a pair of deeply set puppy dog eyes which drew me in when we first met. Even though he doesn't have the flair of Mr STI, or the humour of Mr Summer Fling, despite the distance he pursued me relentlessly, sending thoughtful cards in the post, until I agreed to go on a date with him.

We met up a month later at his friend's house party in Derbyshire, and I was surprised by how much I enjoyed myself. It felt good to be sociable again, and to be the centre of his attention. Having had my trust broken so many times, I got the sense that Steve was loyal, if a tad dull, but that he would never betray me. Only now, as I don a pair of rubber gloves and scrub away his skid marks in the toilet bowl, does it dawn on me: perhaps I hardly know him at all?

Throughout the evening, while I clean every surface, fold and put away his clothes, make the bed and rustle up something for a late supper, I think about what my grandparents would do. Brought up in the pre-war generation, if ever there was a couple who faced hardship and fought on, it's Grandad and Granny Fenwick. I've only ever known my grandparents on my mother's side, so they're both extra special to me.

'Once you've made your bed, you must lie in it,' is what my granny would say if she could see the mess I'm in.

'Only after I've friggin' made it first!' I mentally shout back.

Chapter 4

On Monday morning, I rise with the larks and trudge downstairs into the archaic lean-to bathroom, complete with avocado-coloured suite and accessed from the back of Steve's kitchen, and turn on the hot tap. Waiting for the tub to fill, my feet freeze on the cement floor, forcing me back upstairs and under the bedcovers while it takes the clapped-out boiler thirty minutes to dribble out its contents into the ancient metal tub. Two hours later and turned out in my pristine new uniform, I arrive at my new workplace.

I was delighted to secure this job in Swindon. Having come through my company's Graduate Recruitment Programme means it's easy to transfer roles when new openings appear, and although this is a sideways move from my previous employment in my home city of Newcastle-upon-Tyne, this job comes with more autonomy. If all goes well, I can use this position as a springboard in my career.

Our client's HQ, where I'll be based, is an enormous glass and steel structure on the outskirts of Swindon. A forty-minute commute from Steve's—a journey I'd double checked on my trusty A-Z last night after the confusion the day before—I sign in at reception before my new manager, Mark, comes to collect me.

"Good morning, Victoria. It's nice to see you again." He shakes my hand in greeting. I've met him only once before. During my interview.

"Likewise," I reply.

"Everything work out okay with your move down south?"

"Absolutely. Still a few boxes to sort. You know how it is. But essentially I'm all settled in." I refrain from telling him about the blazing row Steve and I had yesterday after I'd complained further about his slovenly ways. How was I so blind to the mess before?

'If you're not happy, then why don't you bugger off back up north,' he'd said.

'Is that what you want me to do?'

'No, of course not. But I can't have you turning into a hideous nag. On at me if I leave a cup unwashed.'

'Then don't leave a dirty cup unwashed. Do the dishes when they need doing. I don't think it's unreasonable to want to live in basic standards of cleanliness, Steve. Do you?'

He'd walked away, and we'd spent the rest of the day ignoring each other, falling asleep facing away from each other.

"Great," Mark says as he leads me down a corridor. "Well, let's get you settled in here, too. I'm sure you're keen to meet your other colleague."

Turning a corner into our designated office, I spy a couple of feet sticking out from underneath one of the desks. Mark is a local guy. Middle-aged and, judging by the photograph on his desk, married with a couple of teenage sons

"Don't mind the IT guys," Mark says. "They're almost done connecting the switchboards and monitors."

"They look brand new," I say, noticing that these screens are in colour, unlike the black and green DOS based computers I've used previously.

"That's because they are. All mod cons. We've invested heavily in this new contract. It's a great coup for our company. So no pressure then." He laughs.

"No pressure," I repeat, trailing my fingers across the desk that already has my newly printed name plate positioned on it. Sliding into my office chair I start rummaging through my new drawers, emptying the pens and calculator I've brought with me into the top drawer. A slim brunette, around the same age as me, and wearing the same uniform, backs through the office door, arse first, a tray of mugs in hand.

"I don't know how everyone takes their tea yet, so I've kept the milk and sugar separate."

I sit up straight and plaster a smile on my face. This must be the other member of our little team.

"Perfect timing," Mark says. "Victoria Turnbull, meet Melanie Williams."

"Nice to meet you," the brunette says, placing the tray on the corner of my desk and extending her hand.

"Likewise," I reply, taking her hand and consciously gripping it. You can tell a lot by the strength of someone's handshake, and I want to make a good first impression. "Is that an Australian twang I detect?"

"Close, but no. I'm from Christchurch. New Zealand."

"Oh, I'm so sorry," I reply, worried that I've offended her. Similar to mistaking Canadians for Americans, I know how sensitive the Kiwis can be if you mistake them for Aussies. It's a matter of national pride.

"Don't be. It's a common mistake," she says, brushing away my faux pas with a flick of her hand. Milk?" she asks, pouring it into my tea after I nod gratefully. She holds out a spoonful of sugar and I nod again. She stirs the waterfall of white granules into the steaming liquid, before adding a sprinkle more with a cheeky wink. I can tell we're going to get along.

"I've never been to New Zealand, but I hear it's beautiful," I say, taking the mug of tea from her.

"It is. Both the people and the place. You should go one day."

"Well, now I've met you, perhaps I will."

As dedicated Business Travel Consultants, Melanie and I are to be the engine room of the onsite travel office. We will be doing the day-to-day work required to service our client's complex and busy business travel needs. As a global energy provider with offices and investments all over the planet, it's our job to get their employees to the right country, with the right visa and currency in their pockets and in time for their impossibly tight business schedules. However, the size of the account doesn't justify Mark's presence full-time, so he is to split his days between this office and a couple of similar-sized accounts dotted in and around Swindon, meaning day-to-day Melanie and I will be left to our own devices.

"Between the pair of you, you have full responsibility for office security, the foreign currency in the safe, and all the blank airline tickets," Mark briefs us, as he goes through the process of issuing office keys and formally inducting us. "I don't need to remind you how important these are." Using a pen knife, he rips into a box of the perforated airline tickets that we feed into our ticketing printer each day, before being locked away again each evening. "It only takes a couple of keystrokes to print off a first-class ticket to anywhere in the world."

"Oh, don't tempt me," Melanie quips, wrinkling her nose while Mark turns away, presumably so he can deny culpability if anything untoward were to happen on his watch.

Melanie and I agree our work pattern of split shifts to cover the 8:30 a.m. to 6:00 p.m. office opening hours, before we spend the rest of our first day introducing ourselves to various departments within the sprawling building.

"Did you see the look on his face?" Melanie rolls her eyes. "I don't think our boss has figured out my sense of humour yet. Here, which one do you want?" She points to the plate of cupcakes in her hand. We're hoping that a sugary bribe will smooth over the transition from the previous incumbent supplier.

"But we can't Melanie. They're for the clients."

She picks up the biggest cake on the platter. A chocolate one, piled high with brown frosting and dusted with shavings of chocolate flake. "Says who?" she mumbles, her mouth already full of chocolate sponge, a moustache of buttercream on her upper lip. "And from now on, call me Mel. Only my mother and my older sister insist on calling me Melanie."

I stifle a giggle, select a pink cupcake and stuff it into my mouth. The sweet strawberry flavour neutralises the sour taste I've had on my tongue for the past forty-eight hours. "Alright then, Mel. And you must call me Vicky, otherwise *you* sound just like *my* mother."

"Cool," she says easily, and the heaviness I've felt in my chest these past two days lifts ever so slightly.

Part Two

Chapter 5

September, 1993

Over the next eighteen months, my life settles into a dichotomy of polar opposites. Unremarkable domesticity living with Steve, and fun, challenging work alongside Mel. After my disastrous first weekend moving in with Steve, we reached an uncomfortable truce which in reality means I do the bulk of the housework and he pays the bulk of the bills. He works long hours at a stressful job, but then so do I, and what little time I have for me is spent keeping the wheels of our domestic life turning. At weekends, rather than heading into Bath or Swindon for a pub crawl, we head off for long country walks, making the most of our National Trust membership. It's a quiet life, but then it's also a life without any drama.

"Pray tell, what outrageousness did you get up to this past weekend?" I ask Mel as I walk into the office carrying two fresh mugs of tea one Monday morning in September. Hunched over her compact mirror, she's attempting to rub away yesterday's smudged eyeliner from the bottom of her lids.

"Oh my God. It was an absolute riot." She throws her head back and laughs, taking the steaming mug from me.

"Go on," I encourage.

"It was Mich's housewarming on Saturday. I remember nothing past midnight, until I woke up in a freezing cold bath."

Michelle, or Mich to those close to her, is Mel's older sister. She lives up in London, and after following in her father's footstep with a career in the navy, she's now a shipbroker in the City. Like Mel, she works hard and plays equally hard.

"Jesus, Mel. How did you end up naked in a freezing cold bath? You could have caught hyperthermia," I ask, my eyes wide.

"Oh, don't be such a prude Vicky. It was empty, and I had my clothes on. I must have stumbled in there at some point, deciding it was the most comfortable place to crash."

Mel recounting the tales of her crazy social life and weekend antics has become part of our Monday morning ritual. As a second generation Kiwi, she has plenty of cousins and distant 'rellies', as she calls them, scattered around the country. There aren't enough weekends in the year to fit in all the social events she's invited to.

"God, you must have had a bad head the next morning," I continue.

She shrugs. "Some of us took a picnic down to Greenwich. That soon cleared away the cobwebs."

"So when did you get back?"

"This morning. It got so late yesterday evening it wasn't worth driving back last night, so Tim and I left early this morning and he dropped me straight here."

Tim is Mel's landlord-come-male-best-friend. An accountant by trade, after the breakup of his marriage, he rents out the extra rooms in his house to a few young professionals, including Mel. Over the past year the pair seem to have teamed up – if not romantically, then as BFFs. His desire for a packed social life seems to match Mel's.

"And how is Michelle's new pad?"

"Fab. Right in the centre of town. Only a fifteen-minute tube ride to the City. Much better than her previous ninety-minute commute from Richmond." She pauses and takes a slurp of tea. "What about you? What did you get up to over the weekend? Anything exciting?"

"Oh, you know." I look down into my mug, my eyes following a solitary bubble that swirls on the surface. "Just the usual."

"Wait, don't tell me." She closes her eyes and pinches the bridge of her nose. "You went clubbing, danced all night and slept on a park bench."

I let go of the breath I didn't realise I was holding.

"No, it's coming to me now," Mel continues. "You went water-skiing at South Cerney, gate-crashed a party at the boat house and ended up dancing on the tables."

I meet her gaze. "You know none of that happened, Mel."

"You're right – I know you didn't. Because every Monday morning, it's the same story. Friday night, you cooked Steve his tea. Saturday you went food shopping, followed by a day of housework, rewarding yourself with a bottle of wine watching whatever crap was on the telly in the evening. Sunday you spent ironing Steve's shirts for the following week, and – if you're lucky – maybe you pushed the boat out with a long walk to some crusty old tea room on Sunday afternoon. The most exciting thing you've done this past year is go to the Royal Bath Agricultural show. And I can't say a day out trudging through stalls of livestock and potted jams is my idea of fun. Not when you're our age, Vicky."

Avoiding her glare, I swallow down the lump in my throat. This is not how I imagined my life would turn out when I left the North-East and leapt into a life with Steve. All the adventures I thought we'd go on, the unstoppable team we would become, when the reality couldn't be farther from my dreams.

"Sorry." Mel's pulls down the corner of her lips. "I don't mean to be harsh, but you act like you're in your forties. I want to make as many memories as possible in my twenties. Do all the crazy things you don't have the freedom to do once you're older. I just think you should be out having fun, Vicky. Getting pissed, running naked across someone's lawn in the dead of the night and not caring where you crash."

"Even if it's in a bathtub."

"Exactly. Make Steve iron his own bloody shirts and cook his own tea. He's not a baby. If you're not careful, you'll look back and realise your life never got started before it's over. All I'm saying is you and Steve should let loose once in a while. Do it now, before you're tied down with kids and a mortgage."

"I would love to spend my weekends gallivanting all around the country like you do, but Steve is so set in his ways."

"But didn't you tell me you two used to hang out with friends and stuff – before you moved in together? What happened?"

"I don't know. He prefers to stay home these days. He seems content. Happy with the way things are."

"And what about your happiness?"

I shrug.

"And have you tried telling him how you feel?"

"I have. But he doesn't seem to get it." My mind flicks back a conversation over dinner a few nights ago.

'Are you happy Steve?' I'd asked.

Holding his fork in mid-air, he's stopped and looked at me. His eyebrows knitted together in confusion. 'What an odd thing to say? You are funny Victoria. Of course, I'm happy. Why wouldn't I be?'

'I'm not sure. I just wondered if you ever thought… is this it? Or if there's more – to life I mean?'

'You are a strange one,' he'd put down his fork and laughed. *'What more is there? I mean, we're happy, aren't we?*

'I guess.'

'Well then. What are you worrying about?'

And that was it. Conversation over and he'd carried on eating, oblivious to my deeper needs or the reasons behind my questions.

"I've never really thought about it." I lie to Mel. "I'm not unhappy, per se. More… stuck. Like I'm waiting for something to kick-start my life."

"Or someone?" she questions, her eyebrows raised. "If you're not happy, you can just leave him, you know."

I jerk my head backwards. "But why would I do that? Steve loves me."

Mel presses her lips together into a thin line and returns her attention to her computer screen. "It's your life, Vicky. I'm just saying."

She's right. It is my life and it may not be the exciting and adventurous crazy life that Mel leads, but at least I'm in a relationship with a guy who loves me. Isn't that what everyone wants? To be loved. Even if it means giving up some things you once dreamed of. Surely nothing is ever worth more than being loved?

Chapter 6

A couple of months later, when Mel and I are once again offloading our respective weekend news, she shakes her head and announces, "Right. That's it. I'm not taking no for an answer. Tomorrow night, you're coming round to Tim's for supper. He's having a few friends over. Nothing formal, but you have to get out and do something. Your craic's bloody appalling and I can't take any more of your boring Monday morning updates."

"I'm not sure, Mel. I need to check with Steve first. I don't know how he'd feel about me going out without him. Who'd cook his tea?"

She squeezes her eyes tight shut, before reopening them and locking her stare onto me. "He's not a toddler, and you're not his prisoner. Surely you're allowed out for one night? Tell him you're my plus-one and that I wouldn't take no for an answer. And you're staying over." She points her index finger in my face. "I'm not having you turn down a glass of wine because you have to drive home. You're bunking in with me and that's that."

I know I should object and list all the reasons I can't go, but a tiny bubble of excitement pops inside my gut at the prospect of doing something different. Maybe some of Mel's self-confidence will rub off on me.

The next day, I arrive at work with an overnight bag and still shaking from the blazing row that had erupted when I'd shared my plans with Steve. Mel is on the later shift, but I stay with her after my shift ends, before we close up the office and head to Tim's smart five-bed new build on the outskirts of town. Mel cranks up the music in her bedroom while we both shower, change and reapply our makeup.

"I can't remember the last time I had a girlie night like this." I pour her a glass of wine. "I think the last time was in the dorms at college, getting ready for the summer ball."

My mind flicks back to the hours before my final university black-tie do and the camaraderie I felt amongst that group of friends. They felt like family, but it's strange how you lose touch once the threads that once bound you are cut. With three siblings, though, I sense Mel's upbringing didn't involve long periods of solitude or loneliness.

Ninety minutes later I'm brushing non-existent crumbs off my stonewashed Levi's. I pull on a military-style boxed jacket over the top of my crisp white shirt and slip oversized gold hoops through my ears. Meanwhile, Mel has teamed her jeans with a batwing style purple top and piled her hair into a messy bun on top of her head. A chunky statement necklace finishes her look.

Making our way downstairs we shuffle onto the stools at the end of Tim's kitchen island and watch while he scoots between the hob, fridge and oven, finishing the last of the prep.

"Looking lovely, ladies." He pulls a fresh bottle from the fridge and pours us each a glass.

I suppress my innate reflex to want to bat away Tim's compliment, and instead accept the glass and the compliment as offered.

"Nice pinny." Mel sniggers.

Tim's apron, worn over his light blue Polo shirt and cream chinos, sports an image of a naked Adonis, complete with rippling six-pack. A strategically placed rolling pin only just covers the model's modesty, and my cheeks flush hot at the implication. It's so… masculine. Tim grips one forearm with his opposite hand and juts out his chin, mimicking a bodybuilder's pose. "It's hard to hide perfection," he says through gritted teeth.

"Hardly," Mel replies a tad too quickly, before gulping down a large mouthful of wine.

Tim's eyes meet hers and his cheeks flush before he turns away and resumes the whipping of his pea foam.

"Apart from my sis, who else is coming tonight?" Mel asks, changing the subject.

Tim checks his Rolex. "If he can get away from work in time, Michelle mentioned that she may drag David along."

David is Michelle's long-term boyfriend. A quiet scientist. They've not long moved in together. Setting up home in her two-bed Russell Square flat.

"Then there are a couple of guys from my work, and one of them is bringing his wife. Together with us three, that makes eight."

"Cool," Mel says.

My bones feel rigid and brittle at the thought of being thrust into such a dynamic social situation. I can't remember the last time I've met so many new people in one go. What if I've forgotten how to behave in a group of people my own age?

"What else needs doing, Tim? Can I help?" I ask, more to calm my nerves than out of a desire to be useful. I was hoping for a night off from domestic duties.

"Mel can." He winks in her direction. "She has to earn her keep, whereas you're a guest under my roof tonight, so your only job is to sit there and look pretty."

Mel tuts like a petulant teenager, jumps down off the stool and inspects one of the pots on the hob. Picking out the wooden spoon, she licks the back of it before dropping it back into the bubbling liquid. "Mmm, delicious."

"Oi," Tim shouts. Using a rolled-up tea towel, he flicks it across her bum. "Keep your stinky paws off my sauce. Make yourself useful and plate up the crudities."

Out in the hallway the doorbell rings, and I jump down off my stool and head to the front door, throwing "I'll get it" over my shoulder before Tim is able to object.

Pulling open the door, I'm expecting to see Michelle and David's friendly smiles, but I'm greeted by a slick of yellow, blonde hair, hanging like a wet curtain over the top of a pair of piercing blue eyes, nestled inside a square face. A drenched arm reaches up like a zombie and offers me a bottle of Veuve Clicquot. Struck mute and failing to notice the rain, I'm blocking the stranger's path.

After an uncomfortable pause, he asks, "Err, hello? May I come in… before I drown out here?"

Like a roll call, I run through the guest list in my head. "Of course. You must be one of Tim's colleagues from work." I take the bottle from him. "Come on in. I'm Victoria. Mel's friend."

I step aside and he leans back, taking an exaggerated Basil Fawlty-esque step over the threshold. "Ah yes. You two work together, don't you? Nice to meet you, Victoria. I'm Jeremy." He peels off his Barbour jacket, shaking the rain off it.

"Here, allow me." I hang his coat with the others and wait while he reviews his reflection in the mirror.

Running his fingers through his hair, it settles back into a preppy schoolboy flick. "It's absolutely atrocious out there. Still, nice weather for ducks."

What a stereotypical British upper-class thing to say, I think, although I stay quiet as his eyes track my movements through the mirror.

"Right then, Victoria." He smiles. "Point me toward the booze."

"Through there."

He waits for me to lead the way, but when I hold back he heads in the direction of my outstretched index finger, and a few seconds later, whilst I continue to loiter in the empty hallway, I hear the whoops and hollers of old friends greeting each other. As usual, I'm one step behind.

"Well, that was absolutely de-lic-ious," Michelle says a few hours later after we've all polished off Tim's scrummy meal of Scallops with Pea Foam, followed by Chicken and Shallots in Red Wine Gravy. She places her knife and fork at an angle on the edge of her plate, then leans back and stretches her arms above her head. "I would ask for sex, but I don't have room."

"Mich!" Mel exclaims.

"Oh, relax. Ever since our little brother came home from school and announced he'd had sex at lunch, and thirds of mashed potato, you know I mean *second helpings*."

Everyone around the table explodes into laughter.

"I'd forgotten about that," Mel says. "How old was he then?"

"Five? Or six, maybe? I can't remember, but it was funny. Speaking of our darling Chris-to-pher..."

I've noticed how Michelle always enunciates her words, emphasising each syllable.

"...I had a letter off Dad this week. He reckons Chris is planning a trip to Europe next year. Wants to tramp around the continent, so naturally he'll use us as a jumping-off point."

"Oh, that'll be nice," I say. Mel often talks about her family, and although both she and her siblings hold dual nationality on account of her British-born father, other than her sister up in London she has seen none of her New Zealand rellies since the last time she travelled home for Christmas.

Mel's eyes soften and she lowers her voice. "It'll be good to have him visit. I've missed him."

"You say that now, but wait until the man-child has emptied your fridge, filled the laundry basket with his crusty undercrackers and shagged all your mates."

The heat of a flush creeps up my neck as the long-legged wife of Tim's colleague sniggers into her wine. Meanwhile, all the men smile, the behaviour of Michelle and Mel's youngest brother clearly resonating with them.

"Trust me," Michelle addresses the room. "As the baby of the family, he got away with murder. I love my little bro, but he can be a right pain in the arse."

"Whereas being the second youngest," Mel says, "he and I were as thick as thieves."

"Always up to mischief, more like," Michelle adds.

"Aren't all siblings the same?" Jeremy says. "My younger brother and I were. Even now we hang out together at least once a week." He smiles sideways at me, inviting me to endorse his comment, but I drop my head and avoid his gaze.

"I'm just about to finish a letter to Mum," Mel says. "I'll ask her if she knows when he's planning on coming over."

"Why don't you write to your brother direct?" I ask, and both Michelle and Mel guffaw with laughter.

"When you meet him, you'll understand," Mel says. "In all the years I've lived abroad, Chris has never written to me. Not once. Not even a postcard. For someone who can talk the hind legs off a donkey, he's useless at putting pen to paper."

"Oh," I mumble, feeling as if I should have been aware of this sibling-esque nuance, and that as an only child I've somehow shown myself up.

The conversation rolls on around me, and as much as I try to remain engaged, Tim is talking to his other colleague about the impact of a recent internal announcement, Michelle has slipped into a private discussion with David, and the Leggy Wife and Mel are discussing a recent film release – *Indecent Proposal,* starring Demi Moore and Robert Redford.

"Have you seen it?" Jeremy leans into me and whispers.

"No." I turn and smile politely. "Have you?"

"Not yet. I haven't found the right person to take."

"Oh?" I raise my chin before dipping it slightly. "Why don't you go anyway? On your own, I mean."

"What a depressing thought." He laughs. "How sad do you have to be to go to the pictures on your own? Come on. I mean, who does that?"

I press my lips inwards and try to suppress the heat that creeps up my neck. There's no way I'm going to admit that I sometimes go to the cinema alone. It's a way to kill a few hours on the Saturday mornings when Steve goes out grouse shooting with his pals and I'm bored with doing housework. When I dissect the details with Mel on our Monday morning catch-ups, I tell a white lie and say Steve and I went together.

"It's a film I'd like to see though." I re-engage Jeremy. "The story sounds intriguing. Voluntarily choosing to sleep with someone for a million bucks, and with your husband's blessing."

"I would never give *my* blessing to that type of transaction. Abhorred. Pimping your wife for financial gain. Eurgh." He shivers and takes a large slug of wine.

"But I guess that's the point of the movie. It forces you to examine your own moral compass. You and I have never been that desperate, so how could we know what we would or wouldn't do?"

"I respectfully disagree. No matter how desperate the circumstances, I would never lower myself to that level."

"Easy to say when you've got family and money behind you," I mutter under my breath.

He raises an eyebrow. "Now who's being judgemental?"

Damn, he wasn't meant to hear that.

"Sorry, that came out sharper than I intended. Let's just hope that neither of us ever have to make such a horrible choice."

"I agree. But you strike me as a woman very much in control of her life. Someone who wouldn't allow herself to be compromised. Regardless of the pay off."

His words hit me like a kick in the gut. Winded, I gasp for air. He reaches for my hand and gives it a gentle squeeze, causing a jolt of electricity to zap through my veins. "In fact, you're just the kind of woman I'd love to take on a date to see *Indecent Proposal*. I'm sure we'd both find the debate afterwards stimulating."

I'm struck mute by his brash declaration, but his lips pull into a smile and, letting go of my hand, he retrieves his napkin off his lap, causing his fingers to brush against my thigh. Even through my jeans, his touch feels hot, as if he's just branded me with his mark. He dabs the corners of his mouth before folding his napkin and placing it next to his side plate, then turning towards me again. But before he says anything else, Tim stands and scoops up a handful of empty plates. I jump up as if my seat pad is on fire, and my chair legs scrape against the floor.

"Let me help," I blurt, gathering up an armful of empties and scuttling behind Tim, feeling the burn of Jeremy's gaze on my back.

"Just dump them there." Tim nods towards the kitchen island. "I'll fill the dishwasher later," he says, plonking down his handful of plates before heading back out of the room. I place my plates next to his pile and turn and lean back against the cool granite worktop. Closing my eyes, I let go of the air in my lungs. My lips pursed like a kiss. When I open them, Jeremy is standing in front of me, his hands laden with more empty tureens. When my eyes meet his, his lips part slightly and he unconsciously touches his upper lip with the tip of his tongue.

Dumping the plates, he reaches inside a cupboard and grabs two crystal tumblers. Retrieving ice from the freezer, he opens another cupboard and pulls out a bottle of Baileys Irish Cream. He clearly knows his way around Tim's kitchen.

"You look like you need a drink." He pours the smooth pale liquid over the frozen cubes which crack and split as the warm cream hits the frigid ice. Without waiting for me to accept, he passes me a glass and chinks his tumbler against the side. "Bottoms up." He holds his drink in front of his face while his eyes dance with mine.

Blinking a few times in quick succession, I shake myself back to life and nod my head in acknowledgement before raising the liquid to my lips, allowing the welcome whiskey and cream mixture to slide over my tongue. It slithers down into my stomach like a tepid snake, and a shiver ripples across my skin.

"Has anyone ever told you, you have the most mesmerising green eyes?" he says.

"Do I?"

"I've never seen anything like them before. Like two sparkling emeralds."

The heat of another flush crawls up my neck. It's been so long since a man has paid me a compliment or showed me any attention, I don't know how to react. Part of me wants to lap up this stranger's adoration, but then on the same level I know the right thing to do is to thank him for the compliment, then cut it dead. I already have a boyfriend waiting for me back at home. But when Jeremy takes a purposeful step forward, I don't stop him; instead, I push my back further into the granite worktop behind me. Without asking, he takes the glass from my hand and places it on the surface next to his.

Oh my god!

Using a finger he tilts my chin towards his. Part of me wants to escape, but I also want to know what his lips would feel like on mine. My eyes drift towards the door. My escape route. But my legs feel leaden and my tongue feels fat and thick and unable to form any coherent sounds. I hold my breath.

No more than ten minutes ago, we were debating the moral dilemma of a married man encouraging his wife to sleep with a rich man to pay off an impossible debt. I wonder what Jeremy's position would be if he were the millionaire in the love-triangle? It would seem that boundary is easier for him to cross.

He closes his eyes as our mouths unconsciously pull towards each other. I too close my eyes.

"There you are." Mel bustles in through the door and Jeremy takes a sharp step back, restoring a respectable distance between us, milliseconds before our lips would have met. Mel pulls a couple of bottles from the fridge. "We thought you'd got lost."

"Not lost," Jeremy answers. "Just chatting."

Seizing the opportunity, I duck past him. "Here. Let me." I take one of the bottles from Mel and, linking my arm through hers, make my way into the dining room.

Out of the corner of my eye I spy Jeremy knock back the remainder of his Baileys, slamming his empty glass onto the counter top, next to my half full one. Meanwhile, I lick my lips, lapping up the last dregs of whiskey and cream on my tongue and a warm glow spreads throughout my body.

Chapter 7

The following day flies by and our in-trays filled with complicated travel requests, Mel and I have no time to dissect the previous evening's events. But when I arrive back home, my heart thuds like a hard stone rattling around an empty tumble dryer. Steve's rented terrace lacks central heating and on cold winter evenings, like this one, I've taken to making up a bed on the hearthrug and falling asleep, shivering, as the embers throw out their final tentacles of heat.

"This is ridiculous," I shout the next morning, pointing at the ice that's formed on the inside of the windows.

Maybe it's the contrast of returning home after such a warm evening at Tim's, but I hear myself scream, "It's the 20th century, Steve. No one should have to live like this. Be a man. Sort it out!"

He stands on the doorstep in tracksuit bottoms and a grubby T-shirt, as I stomp towards my car. "I'm not God. I can't change the weather."

"Figure it out." I slam my car door and floor the accelerator, causing my tyres to spin on the frosty ground.

Driving up the motorway, my mind races along with the traffic. I may have been in love with Steve once, or thought I was, but is it possible I was more in love with the idea of being loved than actually *'in love'* with Steve himself?

Regardless, any affection we once shared has long been buried under the weight of domesticity. But I have no way out. I'm trapped. There's no way I could afford to rent on my own, so if I ended things with Steve, my only option would be to leave my job and move back in with my parents.

I change gear, then, reaching up with my fingers, roll the pads of them over my bottom lip, feeling the plumpness of the flesh I find there. Only thirty-six hours ago, I'd held my breath as Jeremy had almost kissed me. I wasn't sure if I'd wanted him to kiss me, but my body fills with a warm glow as I moisten my lips with the tip of my tongue, imagining what his kiss might have felt like. I may not have invited his pass at me, but I didn't push him away either. Was I simply curious to feel another man's lips on my own? To compare another man's touch to Steve's brusque attempt at affection? A shudder ripples across my skin as I recall the weight of Steve's lumbering body mounting me. Something I've neither instigated nor invited for a long time, now. It's been so long since I've felt anything in that department, I've forgotten what it feels like to soften into the arms of another. Maybe that's why I stood mute in Tim's kitchen. Maybe I was hoping Jeremy's kiss would make the reality of my life disappear – if only for a fleeting moment.

That evening, Steve slides a handful of A4 glossy brochures across the table. I can see they're sales brochures for houses to buy.

"It's too close to Christmas to think about moving," he says, "but maybe in the New Year we should buy somewhere. Together."

A visceral fear rips through me. My fists clench into balls and I hold my breath. This is my fault. It was me, after all, who shouted at him to *sort it out,* when I left this morning. But I didn't mean bloody buy a house together!

Shovelling a forkful of lasagne into his mouth, he continues, "I'm not getting any younger. I'll be thirty-five next year. Maybe you're right. It's time we settle down."

I swallow hard. "Settle down?"

"Yeah, you know. Marriage. Kids. Buying a house. Isn't that what you want?" He points to the brochures that lie untouched on the table between us. "I have enough saved for a small deposit. If we pool our wages, we should be able to get a mortgage for a small starter home. It's about time I got myself on the property ladder."

His lips pull into a featureless smile while he waits for me to respond, but once again I feel as if my life is a runaway train hurtling towards a broken viaduct, about to fall into a ravine. The original picture I'd imagined when I drove south eighteen months ago, of us standing at the altar surrounded by our families as we took our vows, now has the potential to become a hideous reality.

"Maybe," I try to keep the conversation light, but my laugh comes out more like a witch's cackle. "I know I told you to sort things out, but I really did only mean – find a way to keep us warm, not rush headfirst into marriage and mortgages."

"Nonsense. I know I can never do any better than you Victoria and I know you feel the same. Maybe it's time we made things official."

I swallow hard. Although I feel metaphorically and financially trapped, at least without a ring on my finger or a babe in my arms I'm still comparatively free. But only if I act now.

The next day, confronted with the actual reality of sliding down a rabbit hole I won't be able to climb out of, is sufficient for me to discuss my problems with Mel over lunch.

"I don't know what to think," I blurt.

"I don't get it. Just leave him." She looks at me sideways. "Based on how you were flirting with Jeremy the other evening, you can't be that serious about Steve anymore."

"I wasn't flirting with him. He was flirting with me."

"Same thing." She shrugs. "You didn't stop him. Don't worry. I'm not judging you. If anything, you deserve a little frivolous fun after your purgatory as Steve's housekeeper. There's plenty of nice guys like Jeremy out there, you know."

"But if I left Steve, where would I live? I'd be homeless. I'm stuck, and don't know what to do."

"Don't know *what* to do, or don't know *how* to?" She raises an eyebrow in question. "In life, I never worry about the *hows.* They always appear once you decide what you *want.*" After a brief pause, she presses me. "So what do you *want,* Vicky?"

I don't miss a beat, almost shocking myself. "I don't *want* to be with Steve anymore." I suck in a deep breath. "But it's hopeless. How can I leave him? I'd have to give up this job and move back home – and we all know the state of the job market in the North-East. Plus, I'm not sure I could stomach living back home. I left under such a dark cloud."

"So, what are you going to do?"

She waits while I continue processing my thoughts. Dropping my head into my hands, I fight back tears and swallow down the burn at the back of my throat. "I have no idea."

I turn and meet her gaze. She smiles and I see a spark of light in her eyes. It's the same spark that I covet. I know then that I can't stay with Steve. Not if I want my eyes to sparkle like Mel's. I have to leave him. Slamming my palm on my desk, it slaps like a thunderclap. "Alright then. I'll leave him. Even if I have ab-sol-utely no idea how the heck I will do it, or where I am going to live."

"Great. So, here's an idea. Why don't we get a place together?"

I stare at her open-mouthed as a new life path opens up in front of me, offering me the *how* I'd been waiting for. Clearly this was a test. She wanted to know I was committed before she offered me a viable solution to my problem.

"Attractive." She laughs. "Didn't anyone tell you it's rude to stare with your mouth open?"

"Sorry, it's just that that's one option I'd never even considered."

"Tim's just landed a promotion and is moving up to London, and sometime soon will put his house on the market. Once it sells, I'll have to find somewhere new to live anyhow. If I know we're going to bunk in together, I'll give him notice. I'm sure there's a nice two-bed flat out there with our names on it."

This time the tears that prickle at the corner of my eyes are tears of relief.

"See, I told you." Mel bites into her sandwich. "Never worry about the *hows.* Decide first and the *hows* will appear."

I suppose having backpacked halfway around the world, sorting somewhere new to live seems far less daunting to Mel than to me.

"But are you sure? What if we fall out?"

"Then we'll work it out. I think we've worked together long enough to know what winds each other up. I reckon it'll be fun."

"Okay, let's do it." Suddenly, I'm flooded with energy.

"Great. When do you think you'll tell him?"

I stop and ponder this question. Having had no plan only moments earlier, my mind is racing with the intricacies of how I'm going to pull this off. "I'll plan to leave him in six weeks. Just before Christmas. That way I can use the holidays to drive some of my stuff back home. Store it in my mam's attic. Does that work for you?"

"Perfect. I only have to give Tim four weeks' notice."

"Cool. That should give us enough time to find somewhere new to rent. Plus, I don't think I could stomach another Christmas with his folks. As nice as they are, I can't pretend to play happy families. What if he drops a surprise proposal?"

"Shit. Do you think he's planning to?"

"I wouldn't put it past him. He seems dead set on steamrolling me into a future with him. No matter how much I try and tell him, he's oblivious to how I'm feeling."

"Well then. That's settled. I'll talk to Tim tonight, then we can start looking for somewhere to rent."

I finish munching on my tuna baguette and for the first time in months look up at the world beyond my office window. A red-breasted robin sits on a barren tree branch, chirping away. The watery winter sun shining bright in the clear blue sky. A perfect crisp winter's day. My heart lifts and I have hope that my life is about to move in a positive direction. Finally, it feels as if my life is about to get started. For real.

Buoyed by my secret plan, I skip into Steve's kitchen the next morning before stopping dead in the doorway. He stayed up late last night, watching some weird noir thriller and coming to bed long after I'd fallen asleep. My eyes scan the room. Every bench is strewn with dirty dishes, and his overflowing ashtray gives off a stench of stale cigarette smoke which hangs like a fog in the air. Releasing a heavy sigh, I lean over the carnage and open the bread bin.

"Steeeeeeeve, you fucking twat!" I scream, my gasket finally blowing. "There's no fucking bread in the bread bin. You scoffed the last slice and didn't bother to get a new loaf out of the freezer."

"What's going on?" Steve appears, bleary-eyed, at the top of the stairs, scratching his head with one hand and his balls with the other. Dressed only in his boxers, his semi-horn visible through the gaping hole at the front, even though I'm shaking from the adrenaline coursing through my veins I can't be bothered to fight. What would be the point?

"Never fucking mind. I'll get some breakfast at work. And clean up your fucking mess." I slam the door extra hard as I leave.

"I can't take it anymore," I say to Mel once I'm in the office. "I'm sick of picking up after him. He's so inconsiderate. I know I like things neat, but he makes no effort. It's like nothing that matters to me, matters to him, and he has no idea how invisible that makes me feel."

"Finally..." Mel passes me a fresh mug of tea. "Well, you don't have to stay there a moment longer. Here's what we're going to do."

Together we hatch a plan for me to take a sick day and return home once Steve will have left for work. Mel clears it with Tim that I can crash with her until we've found somewhere new to live. It'll be tight, cramming all my stuff into Mel's room, but Tim has said I can store whatever I need in his garage, until we get ourselves sorted.

After I've moved all my stuff up to Tim's, I return to Steve's cottage and sit quietly in the lounge, listening to the ticking of the clock on the wall. Dressed in my winter coat – why should I clean the hearth and light the fire when I won't be spending another night under this roof – I light a candle instead. At least the flickering of the flame gives me something to focus on while I listen to the minutes pass agonisingly by.

I hear his car pull up outside and my body starts to shake. I sit on my hands to keep them still.

His key turns in the lock and he drops his bag by the front door before his mind registers that something has changed. He may not have noticed the pictures on the walls previously, but he's noticing the bare patches now. The house stripped of all my influence.

"Why are you sitting in the dark?" he asks.

I stand up, forcing my shoulders back, attempting to appear more confident than I feel. "I'm leaving you." I point to a pile of paperwork on the coffee table. "I've left a cheque for my half of the rent and utilities for the next four weeks. After that it's up to you what you do."

He stares back at me, his eyes out on stalks. Despite my recent attempts to share with him how empty I've been feeling, I've never threatened to leave before now.

"What do you mean, you're leaving me? I thought we loved each other? This can't be just because I ate the last slice of bread last night. Is it?"

Anger simmers in my blood. How could he be so immune to my needs? I've tried to tell him. I truly have and I'm buggered if he's going to make this all about him. He's not the victim here.

"Steve, I'm sorry, but as you can see, I've already moved out. You don't want a girlfriend, you want a housekeeper, and I've had enough of cleaning up after you. I have no desire to be a middle-aged housewife before my time. I want more. I want a man who makes me feel like a woman, not someone who makes me feel like their mother."

He flops down into his favourite armchair as if he's been blown over.

"But you can't leave me. I love you. And I know you love me too."

There it is again. The constant presumption as to how I am feeling.

Steve, I've realised, sees and believes what he wants to be true and ignores anything that doesn't fit with that reality. I look into his eyes and all I see is a frightened little boy looking back at me. I've said enough. He's so far off the mark there's no point trying to correct him. "Steve. You're blind and there really is no point discussing this anymore. Goodbye, and please say goodbye to your family for me. They've always been very decent to me."

I decide I'll write to his mother, even though I suspect she'll toss any letter from me straight into her fire.

"I've left my key on the side in the kitchen. Goodbye."

I wait for him to respond, but instead he rises from his chair and walks into the kitchen, turning his back on me. His final act of denial or defiance, I'm not sure which. But I don't care. I'm free!

Outside, I suck in a lung-filling breath, lean back against the door and gaze skywards. A bright full moon peeks out from behind the thin threads of clouds that cross the early evening sky. The dark clouds in the foreground hide the pure white light of the moon behind and I feel as if the ominous sky holds meaning. As if it's saying, *Hang in there, Victoria, because behind the clouds, brightness is coming.*

"I sincerely hope so," I whisper back. Second only to leaving my family home, this is the most momentous decision I've ever taken. I hope I'm not making another monumental mistake.

Steve wasn't exciting or dynamic, but he was stable, and despite his slobbish ways I doubt he would ever have cheated on me.

Driving back up the motorway, back towards Mel and my uncertain future, the moon breaks free from the clouds and illuminates the road ahead. Maybe it's an omen. Maybe everything will turn out okay.

I crank up the car stereo and sing along at the top of my voice. *Relight my fire...*

Part Three

Chapter 8

March, 1994

A couple of weeks after my escape from Steve-dom, or as Mel likes to refer to it, *Steve-doom,* Mel and I rented a small but modern two-bedroom semi-detached house (with toasty central heating!) in a small village on the opposite side of the motorway from where we work. We joined the gym at our local Marriott and spend most evenings popping along for a soak in the Jacuzzi, or sweating it out in the gym. I've never been in better shape, mentally or physically.

Melanie is a tall, natural brunette, and very trim, which previously I'd thought was down to genetics, but having lived together for four and a half months, I see how well she takes care of herself. Most evenings she munches on chicken salad or cooks a lean meal from scratch. Takeaways and fast food are rare.

"It's only so I don't feel guilty splurging at the weekends. Life is all about balance, Vicky. Work hard, but play equally hard. That's my motto," she said, when I questioned her about her habits.

And splurge we do. Most weekends we head up to London to hang out with her sister or with Tim, who has purchased a swanky pad on the river at Surrey Quays, overlooking Canary Wharf.

"Is there anything between you and Tim?" I asked, one Wednesday evening when we're slobbing out in front of the telly.

"Why do you ask?"

"Oh, I don't know. I just sense a spark between you two."

"Nope. Nothing to report there."

As well as partying with Tim and Michelle, we occasionally head down to South Wiltshire to visit the family Mel used to au pair for: the Grays. The mum, Margaret, is especially welcoming when Mel introduces me. A small, rotund, bustling woman, she has a warm heart and an open door. Which is just as well, as whenever we visit there seems to be a steady stream of visitors letting themselves in and plonking themselves around her kitchen table, helping themselves to tea and cake. Including a handsome young farmer named John who always seems to appear when Mel and I turn up.

In the past few months I've also taken Melanie north to meet my family too. However, being such a long way, it's not a trip we can take often.

After eighteen months of purgatory, I have filled the first few months of 1994 with people, parties, and fresh adventures, and I'm relishing every second.

"How about Istanbul?" Mel asks, looking over the top of her monitor one Thursday morning in March. "The loads look good and the flight times work. Leaving tomorrow night from Heathrow and returning late Sunday?"

One of the major bonuses of working in travel is our access to cheap flights. As certified travel agents, we qualify for a seventy-five percent discount on all worldwide airfares, or what's known in the industry as an AD75. We're not highly paid, so Mel and I take advantage of every perk on offer.

If we have no weekend plans, it's not unusual for one of us to log into our flight booking system on a Thursday morning and check seat availability for the upcoming weekend. Flying on AD75s means travelling on a standby ticket, so being bumped on an outward journey is an inconvenience, but ending up stranded abroad on a Sunday night means being late for work the next morning, which even though not technically our fault, is something that is seriously frowned upon.

"Istanbul?" I'm surprised by her choice, and curious. "I've never even considered it before. It's not somewhere we'd likely choose for a proper holiday, but I bet it's fascinating. Perfect for a cheeky weekend getaway. Why not? Let's do it."

Thirty hours later Mel and I are boarding a Turkish Airlines jet to Ataturk. The flight attendant pulls us to one side when we board. Crossing out the seat numbers on our boarding cards, he points to the front two seats 1A and 1B. The front row of the Business Class cabin. Another perk of working in the industry. The tall male flight attendant is wearing black trousers with creases sharp enough to cut paper, and black patent shoes so shiny you can see your face in them. Once we're seated, he offers us two complimentary glasses of champagne.

"Ladies," he says, dipping his tray, allowing us to pick off the long-stemmed glasses. "Compliments of Turkish Airlines."

Giggling like pre-pubescent schoolgirls, Mel and I tap our glasses together. The liquid tastes sour and cheap, but it's free, so we drink it anyway.

"Anything else you need, I'm going to be right here." The attendant smiles and points to the galley two paces behind him.

"That's very kind, Aslan." Mel squints, reading the name badge pinned to his waistcoat.

"Like the lion?" I ask.

"Like the lion," he repeats, stepping back to allow more passengers to board, but not before miming a lion's roar with his free hand.

Sniggering into her champagne, Mel says, "This has the promise to be one of our maddest weekends away yet."

"Let's hope so."

"Who knows? Maybe some highly eligible bachelors will sweep us off our feet."

"Well, judging by the middle-aged pot-bellied passengers boarding this flight, they're not sat behind us," I say, a fraction too loud, causing some of the middle-aged pot-bellied passengers behind me to shuffle uncomfortably in their seats.

"Vicky. You're a disgrace."

"Maybe. But have you noticed, we're the only people under forty on this flight, and there're no women. Weird? I doubt we'll bump into any stag dos this weekend. I don't think Istanbul has made it onto the barmy army's list of weekend breaks."

"Thank heavens. Give me a sophisticated local any day," Mel says before draining her glass. Like lightening, Aslan minces forward and tops her up.

A couple of hours later, as Aslan is clearing away our meal trays, he leans over and whispers, "Ladies. The captain has asked whether you would like to join him and the co-pilot in the cockpit for landing?"

"What?! And sit on their laps," Mel exclaims.

"It's not exactly protocol," he whispers, "but there are two jump seats in the cockpit you're welcome to strap into. If you've never been to Istanbul before, there is no better way to introduce you to her than seeing her lights twinkle before you land."

"We'd love to," Mel and I reply together.

"Okay." He winks. "I'll come and get you when it's time."

We sit back and sip our champagne, and after the familiar *bing* of the seat belt sign being illuminated, Aslan gives us the nod. Opening the cockpit door, he puts his index finger to his lips, before showing us where to sit. Once we're secure, he blows us an exaggerated kiss and closes the door behind him.

The cockpit is pitch black except for the myriad of buttons and levers illuminated across the instrument panel. The pilot and co-pilot are concentrating and don't acknowledge us, but through the glass window, directly ahead and uninterrupted, is a panoramic view of the city. Its lights twinkling magically below, just as Aslan said they would be. A spider's web of fairy lights that snake and twist their way through the ancient streets.

Mel looks over at me and mouths, *'Oh my God.'*

'I know,' I mouth back.

The co-pilot is talking into his mouthpiece, his concentration absolute; the captain, however, turns around and beams at us. His gleaming white teeth reflecting off the light that shines out from control panel.

"Ladies," he drawls, his eyebrows raised as his eyes scan the length of Mel's legs. "So pleased you could join us."

Part of me wants to ask whether he shouldn't be concentrating on the imminent landing, but he exudes an air of such unquestionable authority, I keep schtum.

"The pleasure is all ours," Mel replies.

She leans forward and offers him her hand to shake. Twisting around in his chair he takes it, but instead of returning her handshake he rotates her wrist and kisses her palm. Mel dissolves into giggles.

Turning back around, the captain looks out at the view and points down at the black void in the middle of the city. "That down there, ladies, is the mighty Bosphorus," he says in an accented voice, "and over there, the Golden Horn."

I know almost nothing about Istanbul, even though I've sent clients here on business before, so I listen eagerly to this impromptu aerial tour.

He extends both arms, emphasising the two sides of the city. "This indent in the Earth's crust is the exact point where Asia and Europe collide. The west of the city is Europe, the east, Asia." He claps his hands together. "A melting pot of eastern promise and western influence. There is nowhere else like it in the world."

"Oh my goodness. Is that the Blue Mosque?" Mel shouts, forgetting our instructions from Aslan to remain quiet.

The captain throws his head back and laughs. "Yes. Yes it is."

I crane my neck and glimpse the six, fluted, pencil-shaped minarets that surround the iconic dome just before it disappears under the belly of the plane.

"Not long now, ladies. There's the runway," the captain says, pointing dead ahead at two symmetrical lines of white lights, laid out to the side of the airport terminal.

The co-pilot levels the plane and a few minutes later we touch down and begin taxiing towards the gate.

"That was incredible. Thank you," I say, leaning forward to shake both their hands.

"A once in a lifetime opportunity. How can we possibly thank you?" Mel adds.

"Well, you could join us for a drink," the captain suggests, his eyes never leaving Mel's face.

Mel and I glance sideways at each other. We're not idiots. We've worked in the travel industry long enough to know this invitation is laced with expectation. Of course we want to have some fun this weekend, perhaps even some light-hearted flirtations, but we want to experience the culture and uncover the city's hidden gems, not spend half our time holed up in some mid-range hotel bar with two middle-aged (and likely married) guys we'll never see again.

"That's very kind of you," I say. "However, we just want to get our heads down tonight. It's been a long week. You understand."

"Of course," he says, a sharp edge to his tone. Turning his back to us, he focuses his attention on the clipboard in his hand, clarifying that we're of no further use and our special attention is over.

"Jeez," Mel whispers in my ear. "What happened to asking a girl to dinner before expecting her to put out?"

"Exactly!" I reply, as Aslan reappears at the cockpit door.

Neither of them acknowledge our departure as we follow Aslan back into the glaring light of the cabin. Our first Turkish adventure well and truly over.

Chapter 9

The next morning we jump in a cab to Sultanahmet Square, in the oldest part of the city. Opening the taxi door, an onslaught of chaos hits us like newborn babes emerging from the womb into a room full of light and loud noises. Car horns honk, drivers gesticulating wildly as they cut each other up. Sirens and flashing blue lights cut through the traffic. Groups of men stand on the pavement, smoking and laughing. Meanwhile, the sound of the Adhan calls out overhead, inviting the city to prayer. Even the smell of the city assaults our nostrils. Hot dust, exhaust fumes and the aroma of exotic spices, mixed with the smell of unwashed sweaty bodies and sewage.

I dab my brow as the heat of the morning sun pushes up the mercury, causing damp patches to form in the armpits of my white Laura Ashley linen maxi dress.

"Where to first?" Mel says, turning a full three-sixty on the spot.

The streets are lined with small canopied shops and independent mini-marts. This city appears to have been saved from the influx of western brands that are eroding the cultural essence of so many places around the world. This city feels exactly as it might have done five hundred years ago in the Byzantium era.

"Shopping first," I reply. "Then maybe we can find somewhere for a famous Turkish massage. It's been a tough week at work."

"Good idea. I think they call it a hammam. Maybe we can find someone local who can point us in the right direction."

If we thought the city streets outside were chaotic, stepping inside the Grand Bazaar the pandemonium only intensifies. The domed gold, blue and purple ceiling acts like a megaphone to all the haggling taking place inside. Miniature stalls, selling everything from perfume, strange-looking food, Turkish slippers and all kinds of delicacies are rammed in together, their owners' arms reaching over the top of their counters to argue over prices and exchange Lira for white, plastic-bagged goods.

"We need to find something for our *Illustrious Shelf of Tat,"* I say.

The *Illustrious Shelf of Tat* is a joke between Mel and I, where we would buy each other rubbish souvenirs – plastic Eiffel Towers, stuffed donkeys with ears poking out from straw sombreros, stuffed Loch Ness Monsters – presenting them to each other after our respective trips away. It's part of our job, to go on 'fam trips', or familiarisation trips hosted by airlines and hotels that attempt to smooze us, in the hope we'll recommend their brand over their competition. Since moving in together, we've combined our collection which now takes pride of place on a shelf in the living room.

Strolling through the maze of twisting alleyways, we linger at various stalls, and as much as we're trying to remain inconspicuous it's not long before we have a trail of locals in our wake. We appear to be the only unaccompanied women wandering around town. The fact we are Hijab-less also suggests we are not local, or at least not Muslim, and therefore we stand out from the mix of local men and middle-aged tourist couples.

I've only experienced this type of uninvited attention once before: while on holiday with my parents in Bali for my twenty-first birthday. We were visiting a local Hindu temple, and a crowd encircled me, all wanting to touch my long blonde hair. Although I'd been taken by surprise, there was a part of my ego that swelled at the unexpected attention, and that's the same sensation I feel now. Powerful… and wanted.

While Mel and I pause, peering at more trinkets, two men approach us.

"Ladies." the taller of the two says. "Your first time in Istanbul?"

Not wanting to give them too much encouragement, I keep my back to them. "Yes, it's our first time."

"Then welcome to Istanbul." He bows deeply. "We're honoured you came."

"That's very kind of you," Mel says, unable to hide the smile that creeps across her face.

"And who gave them the keys to the city," I whisper in her ear.

"Don't be mean. He's just being polite," she whispers back.

"Please allow us to show you around our Grand Bazaar. These stalls too expensive. Only for tourists. Not locals," he says, earning him a hard stare from the old hag behind the counter.

"Oh, here we go," I mutter to Mel. "Let me show you where you should spend your money… which just happens to be my brother's-slash-cousin's-slash-father's shop."

She rolls her eyes. "What's the harm? We've got all day to kill." She links her arm through mine and turns to face the men. "Lead the way, gentlemen."

The taller of the two bows again, his arm outstretched, showing the direction in which we're to walk.

The men guide us through the heart of the Bazaar and to stalls that we would never have found on our own. We snap up some perfume, a pair of silk slippers each, and even though I can't imagine where I will put it – maybe on the floor at the bottom of my bed – I splurge on a luxurious silk rug.

"How can I not? It's so cheap – well, relatively," I say, justifying my decision.

"Are you thirsty?" one of the men asks.

"It's a bit early for alcohol," Mel replies.

"Not alcohol. Tea," the taller of the two says.

Mel and I both shrug and follow the men out into the bright

sunshine where they direct us to a small street café and order a round of Çay tea. The bitter brew slides over my tongue and I grit my teeth against the taste. It isn't what I expected, but in the heat of the day I hadn't realised how thirsty I was.

The four of us huddle around a bistro table, while we sip our tea, and the men ask us about our lives in the UK. We share that we are Travel Agents who organise flights and hotels for the employees of our client. They tell us they have cousins in London who own a restaurant, and give us the details. We tell them we'll check it out.

Both men are devastatingly good-looking. Persian skin, jet-black hair and chiselled cheekbones. The outline of ripped torsos visible through their flimsy silk shirts. Clearly related, we assume they're brothers, or possibly cousins. The taller one has straight hair slicked back. Only a few gelled strands falling softly round his face. The other has more naturally curly hair and looks to be the younger of the two.

"What are your plans for the rest of the day?" Mr Tall, Dark and Handsome asks.

"We were hoping to find a hamman," I reply.

"I know where you go. My cousin owns it. Hidden away. You not find massage anywhere like it in Istanbul. We show you."

"Thank you. That's very kind."

"What about later?" Mr Curly-Haired asks Mel. "You have plans tonight?"

Mel tilts her head towards him. "We'll probably find somewhere to eat, then head to some bars afterwards."

"Our cousin own best restaurant in Istanbul. Traditional. You not find food like it anywhere else."

"What a surprise," I whisper under my breath and Mel giggles. "Well, maybe we'll swing by later, but we can't promise," I add. "It depends where we end up."

Sitting back upright, the two men look at each other, then Mr Curly-Haired grabs a pen and scribbles down an address, which he hands to Mel.

"We be there from eight o'clock. Come and find us. Our cousin never charge us, and most restaurants charge premium to tourists."

"Okay, okay." Mel makes a palaver of folding the note and tucking it into the side pocket of her handbag. "Maybe we'll see you later," she adds, tapping the side of her bag where she's stored the note.

"But thank you for showing us around the Bazaar. And for the tea," I say.

"No problem," Mr Tall Dark and Handsome replies. "It my pleasure."

We finish up our drinks and the men lead us through the winding back streets, until they point down an alleyway where the buildings overhang towards each other, almost blocking out the daylight.

"There." Mr Curly-Haired points to a heavy wooden door at the end.

"What? There?" Mel says. "Are you sure?"

"Trust me. You come out feeling like you float on air."

"Okay then. Nothing ventured, nothing gained. Let's go."

We say goodbye to the men and tumble our way down the alleyway, laden with shopping bags and the small rolled-up carpet I'm carrying under my arm.

"Eight o'clock, remember," Mr Curly-Haired shouts after us. "We see you then?"

"Yeah, maybe." Mel blows him a throwaway kiss.

Chapter 10

I rap my knuckles on the intricately carved door and a small hatch opens, revealing two beady eyes set inside a scowling women's face. Her leathery skin etched with deep disgust. She looks me up and down; what she sees appears to displease her as she shouts something in Turkish that I don't understand.

Leaning back, I whisper, "Didn't realise we'd walked into a Monty Python sketch!"

Mel sniggers behind her hand, which endears us to the Turkish women even less.

"Two massage?" I point back and forth between myself and Mel. "Yes?" I add, hoping the upward inflection in my voice conveys my question.

"Evet, gel," she barks, her eyebrows pulled together like a stitch before the door swings open with an eerie creek. Moving aside, her hand outstretched, she invites us across the threshold and we step forward.

Inside the confined entrance, the *click-clack* of our shoes echoes on the tiled floor. We walk towards the cashier. Another leathery-faced woman who's encased inside a cubicle of wire mesh. She writes a number in Lira on a piece of paper and slides it under the wire, and

Mel and I stare at her scowling face, agog. The price she's written down equates to £2.50 in Sterling.

"Well, either we've stumbled upon the cheapest hammam in town, or we're about to be led into a dungeon and sold as slaves, never to see daylight again!" Mel slides her money through the hole and the woman hands her a small towel, a locker key and a bright orange token in return. I too, give the cashier my Lira and take the towel, key and token as she slides them back under the mesh.

The towels are made of white linen, nothing like the big fluffy bath towels back in our hotel, and they're the size of a regular tea towel. Nowhere near sufficient to wrap around yourself; I can't see how you're meant to use it.

"This is getting more surreal by the minute," I whisper across to Mel, as the cashier points down a corridor with another intricately carved door at the far end.

Creeping through the door, we find ourselves inside a changing room. Old metal lockers line one side of the double height room. Lime wash paint is peeling off the walls like a dried out facemask. Down the centre of the room, a line of plain wooden benches offer the only place to sit. At the far end, a huddle of local women squawk and screech like a gaggle of geese, their conversation amplified by the bare walls in the simple room. I run the back of my hand across my brow. Compared to the dry heat outside on the streets, inside this sweatbox the temperature and humidity is stifling, which may explain why most of the women at the end of the room are either completely starkers or near naked.

One rather buxom woman, with enormous heavy breasts that hang down to her waist, is wearing a pair of black lacy knickers that have a massive hole on one side, so that the dimpled flesh of her right buttock bulges through. Despite their obvious lack of clothing, all the women appear comfortable in their bodies and I assume they must be friends who come here regularly.

Choosing two empty lockers next to one another, Mel and I peel off our clothes, folding and placing them inside, along with our purchases from the Bazaar.

Naked from the waist up, Mel turns to me, her eyebrows raised. "In for a penny, in for a pound?" she says, before whipping off her knickers and throwing them into the locker. Using the postage-stamp sized tea-towel she covers her lower half, leaving her pert breasts bobbing with the swing of her hips. Chuckling at the madness of what we're doing, I follow suit.

Clutching our towels to the front of our torsos, maintaining our modesty as best we can, we follow our noses through the only other door out of the changing room, leaving the locals to jabber away oblivious to both our arrival and departure.

What lies beyond could not be more different from the sparse and dilapidated changing room we've just come from. A luxurious, cavernous chamber, with an enormous domed ceiling, hexagonal in shape, is dominated by a large circular marble slab in its centre. Ornate carvings and stone fountains cover the walls, and a couple of archways lead to cooler anti-chambers to the sides. Mel and I stand dumbstruck and unsure what we're meant to do. Two woman – also naked – are lying on top of the marble slab. Their eyes closed, they appear completely relaxed. My eyes glide over the soft, smooth curves of their lithe limbs which contrast against the shock of pubic hair at the base of their torsos as they lie prostate, comfortable in their nakedness.

"When in Rome 'n all that," Mel says, throwing down her towel and copying the other women.

Hesitating (I've never been naked in public before), I realise I have no choice but to follow suit. Shuffling over to the other side of the slab, I pick a spot, smooth out my tea towel and copy everyone else. Within seconds, I'm drenched in sweat. The marble is hot to the touch, heated, I realise, from a furnace below. The warmth permeates my body, caressing it like the inside of a warm womb. Closing my eyes, I turn my focus inward and take a few deep breaths as I try to block out the fact that I'm lying in a public place, naked. But my body remains tense and stiff. I feel as self-conscious as hell. Heck, I don't even walk around naked in the privacy of my bedroom. Lying on my back, I suck in a few more lung-filling breaths before releasing them slowly.

Sunlight lands on the back of my eyelids and, opening them, my eyes focus on the domed ceiling above. Painted in vibrant hues of blues and golds it is perforated with hundreds of Moorish crosses, allowing beams of light to shine down like shards of glass and giving the humidity a means to escape. Still, the air is saturated with water droplets that shimmer like suspended magical stars. This place feels positively holy and, despite my vulnerability, I feel safe within its walls.

After ten minutes, my skin glistening with sweat, my muscles begin to relinquish their tension. My feet flop outwards as my glutes relax, and I throw an arm over my head, the back of my hand soaking up the hypnotic heat.

"We'd never have found this place in any official guidebook," Mel whispers. "Do you reckon it's for women only? Or do you think any minute now some delicious hunk will walk through that other door?"

"Or knowing our luck, a horrible, hairy pot-bellied man, like the ones on the plane over." I snigger, earning me a hard stare from one of the other women.

"If you could guarantee a Calvin Klein underwear model with an enormous willy, I wouldn't mind him throwing his towel down next to mine," Mel says, patting the area on the slab next to her. "Or he could forget his towel altogether and just lie on top of me."

"Mel!" I exclaim.

This time, the other woman *tsks* her annoyance as she rolls over onto her front. I turn my head at the sound of the changing room door bursting open, but rather than a Calvin Klein hunk, one of the naked Turkish women we'd seen earlier in the loud gaggle strides towards Melanie, who mouths, *'What the fuuuuuuck?'* back over to me.

"Jeton," the woman snaps.

When Mel looks at her blankly, the woman collects the orange token that Mel had brought into the room with her and placed next to her on the slab, and deposits it through a slot in the wall. The woman then gestures for Mel to roll onto her tummy before she rubs oil onto her hands and begins to massage Mel's back.

A-ha, so this is the massage bit of a traditional Turkish hamman. I wonder who I'll get? I try to recall any details from the gaggle in the changing room, realising now they are not visitors, but in fact work here. Not Big Boobs and Ripped Knickers. Please... not Big Boobs and Ripped Knickers, I repeat over and over in my mind like a mantra. I have a feeling she would pummel me like a slab of meat at the butchers; I may not survive her hands pounding my delicate flesh. I hear the side door burst open and, indeed, Big Boobs and Ripped Knickers strides towards me.

"Jeton," she barks, and I dutifully hand her my token. She twirls her fingers and I roll onto my front, groan, and prepare to be annihilated.

One hour later, any misgivings I'd had about this experience have vanished, as Betty Big Boobs (as I've affectionately named her in my head) has just given me the best massage of my life.

First, she'd massaged my entire body. Pulling my limbs with one hand whilst gliding her other over my muscles. Her hands had moved around every part of my body, stretching sinews, now softened in the heat and humidity. She'd dug every part of her fingers, elbows, and arms into my flesh, loosening any knots and releasing any tension she'd found. She'd worked from my scalp to my feet, asking me to turn over so she could repeat the entire process down the front of my body.

Once sufficiently limbered, stretched, and loosened, she'd drawn a bowl of warm water, agitating it first so that the liquid frothed up. Using a muslin cloth, she'd squeezed the soapy suds into the arch of my back. Warm, moisturising suds lathered my skin and dribbled down between my butt cheeks, igniting a spark down there that had felt both shocking and pleasurable at the same time.

Sliding her hands into two large exfoliating mitts, the size of oversized oven gloves, she'd then scrubbed my skin. Holding each limb in turn, she'd exfoliated away the old me and a new, tingling me emerged from beneath her touch. Moving methodically up and down the length of my body, and then, after instructing me to roll onto my back so that my front was now unabashedly exposed, down the length of my torso. I knew my nipples were standing proud, as her massive mitts swirled and moved around the front of my body. Every swoosh and swirl of her hands disconnected me more and more from the external world as I slid behind my eyelids, sliding deeper and deeper into the erotic sensations flooding my core. Every nerve ending electrified as she brushed away the dead me, and a new inner flame sparked into light.

Breathless and off-kilter, once she had finished scrubbing she'd tapped my arm and, gripping my elbow, had led me into an antechamber. Smaller and cooler than The Warm Room, she'd stood me in front of a stone-carved fountain and, using her now empty bowl, tipped fresh water over my head, rinsing away all the residual soap, oil and dead skin. Rinsing away the old me. I no longer felt self-conscious of my nakedness and stood proudly as she'd tipped water again and again over my crown. As the water dribbled in rivulets down my skin, cleansing me, I felt reborn. As if she had baptised me into my body somehow.

Before guiding me back into The Warm Room, she'd pulled her lips into a wide smile, revealing a black gap in the front of her gnashers. Wafting her hand up and down the length of my torso, she'd said in her heavy Turkish accent, "Very nice."

Her words were not sexually motivated, rather a simple compliment from one woman to another.

I'd grown up with such a complex opinion of my body, believing my thighs too big or my boobs too small, that whenever I receive compliments, particularly from the opposite sex, I've become deft in batting them away before deleting them from memory. But today Betty Big Boob's two simple words have smacked me right between the eyes. Maybe it's because I'd spent an hour in her care and she'd left me floating on air, but instead of swatting the compliment away I'd allowed it to land, and smiled meekly and nodded my thanks.

As she'd retreated to the changing room and I'd returned to lie down once again on the marble slab, I'd run my fingertips over my naked form. Tracing the shape of my arms, my shoulders, the curve of my neck, running one hand down the centre of my torso, before I settled my palm over the mound of my pubis as if feeling my body for the very first time.

If a craggy old Turkish masseuse thinks I'm *'very nice'* then maybe, just maybe, I might be, if not nice, then at least okay?

Chapter 11

"You're positively glowing." Mel pinches my bum after we've showered, changed, and we're stepping into the lift a few hours later.

"As are you! I've always loved that dress on you."

"Yes, but you're glowing from the inside."

"We both are. My skin has never felt so smooth. Do you think we could come back here every few months so Betty Big Boobs can scrub me clean again?"

"Now wouldn't that be nice?" She squeezes my hand as the lift doors open and we step out into the hotel lobby.

"Where to first?"

"Seriously?" She crumples her mouth into a wry smile before striding towards the hotel bar. Obviously she intends us to grab a quick drink from the hotel before heading down into town. "Let's see if we can score a freebie. Watch this," she says, sliding onto a bar stool as I take the one next to her. Flicking her auburn waves behind her shoulders, she gives the barman her broadest smile. "Two champagne Bellinis, please."

I watch as she leans forward, placing an elbow on the bar and giving the barman a bird's-eye view of her cleavage. Her eyes track his every move while he prepares our drinks.

Moments later, he places our champagne flutes down on top of two monogrammed napkins. "Two beautiful drinks, for two beautiful ladies."

The barman makes no attempt to prepare a bill and, placing both hands on the bar, waits for Mel to taste the drink.

"Hmmm. Delicious." She licks her lips seductively and the barman's eyes remain locked with hers.

Bending down, giving him an even deeper view of her cleavage, she retrieves her clutch bag and makes to open it, but the barman raises his hand. "It's on the house, ladies. Enjoy your evening."

Turning, Mel chinks her glass against mine. "See what a little harmless flirtation can get you?"

"I don't know how you do it."

"Do what?"

"Flirt. You're so good at it."

Mel shrugs. "It's like riding a bike. Stick with me, Chook, and we'll soon have a plethora of suitors eating out of your hand." She takes another sip of her drink. "And if all else fails, I find flashing a boob always glosses over any awkward lulls in the conversation."

"Mel!" I laugh, my hand flying up to my mouth. "Honestly, I can't take you anywhere."

"Is this seat taken?" a deep voice behind me asks.

I turn towards the source of the dulcet tones and my vision is almost severed by the sharpness of the man's suit and matching waistcoat. No tie, and an open top button. He threads his fingers through his dark hair, peppered grey at his temples, and I spy a Patek Philippe watch glint on his wrist.

Mel gives me a nudge in the ribs and whispers, "Perfect opportunity for you to practise."

"Behave," I whisper back, squeezing her knee. "No. By all means." I hold out my hand, palm upwards, and the businessman settles onto the vacant stool next to me.

"Whiskey sour," he says to the barman, who nods before swinging into action, throwing the bottle into the air where it spins a full three-sixty before he pours the bourbon into the cocktail shaker from a great height.

The man takes a slug of his freshly made drink before letting out an *ahh* through gritted teeth.

"Looks like you needed that. Long day?" I ask.

"You could say that. So, I would ask, *do you come here often?* But I know that's the cheesiest chat up line in the history of chat up lines." His eyes traverse the length of my crossed legs. "And you look like a woman who deserves a lot better."

I splutter into my drink. Bubbles shoot up the back of my nose, but I swallow down my mouthful of Bellini to avoid spitting it all over his lap. "Well, that's very kind of you to say. But I think your attempt to cover up the cheesiest chat up line ever, has resulted in an *even cheesier* chat up line."

We both laugh.

"I can only apologise. Hi, I'm James." He extends his hand and I return his handshake.

"Nice to meet you. I'm Victoria." At the touch of his fingers, an unexpected heat creeps up my neck and I grab another sip of my drink before he notices the change in my complexion. Regaining my composure, I continue, "So James, is that Jim, Jimmy, Jimbo?" I tease, the alcohol in my stomach pushing me to be more daring.

"Just James." He winks, flipping his wallet open and pulling out a two-million Lire note which he slaps down on the silver plate the barman has placed in front of him. I glimpse a photograph of two beaming babies smiling out from the inside cover of his wallet.

"It's ridiculous, isn't it?" I point at the Lira. "Only place in the world where you wouldn't want to be a millionaire."

"Correct. Least valuable currency in the world. But a great place to do business."

"So, Just James, do you come here often? I know, I know. It's the cheesiest chat up line in the history of chat up lines, but I'm genuinely curious." I take a sip of my drink, my eyes twinkling at him over the top of my glass. I'm enjoying myself.

He picks up his drink and I notice he's not wearing a wedding ring. "Sadly, all the bloody time. What about you, Victoria?"

"No, just here for the weekend with my friend." I glance over my shoulder to see Mel deep in conversation with the barman.

"In Istanbul? Strange. I would have thought Paris or Barcelona would have been a more obvious choice for two young women like yourselves. Why here?"

"We often have to travel for work. It's part of our responsibility to make sure the hotels are suitable for our clients."

"Ah, I see." Pausing, as if considering his next words, he continues, "So which other interesting cities have you been to?"

"Oh, all over," I reply enthusiastically, now that we're discussing a topic I have lots of experience in. "Let me think. Over the past few years, since Mel and I began working together, we've been to Lisbon. Bruges. That was fun. We got invited to a private party inside a casino. A lot of money changed hands that night, I can tell you."

He nods in understanding.

"Then there was Strasburg. I went on my own that time. Very different from anything I was expecting. More German than French. Where else?" I rap my fingers against the side of my glass. "Mel's been to Milan. And earlier this year we both went to Amsterdam, obviously."

"Obviously."

"Yes, but I find Amsterdam a bit crass. Too in your face – if you know what I mean."

"I know exactly what you mean. One should always be discreet. No point putting it all out there for the world to see."

"Yes, exactly." I'm warming more and more to Just James. He's so easy to talk to. Clearly here on business, he reminds me of our own business travellers, sent all around the world for work. Away from his family; I can only imagine what a drag it must be for him to be away from home, especially over a weekend. "The rest of the time," I continue, "we hang out in London. Many of our friends are in Finance and work up in the City."

"I see." He knocks back the remnants of his drink.

"So what's your status, Just James? Married. Divorced. Single?"

"It's complicated."

"Isn't it always?"

"Another?" He points at my now almost empty glass.

"Only if you buy my friend one too. I couldn't accept a drink and leave Mel without one."

"So you two come as a pair?" He raises his hand at the barman, who sets about preparing us all another round of drinks.

"Absolutely. Totally joined at the hip. We live and work together."

"Very cosy." He smirks.

"It is. But it works for us," I reply brightly. "Few people could do what we do and live together as well. But we both like doing the same things, so it keeps it simple, plus it's fun."

"I can imagine." His eyes twinkle as he listens, making me warm to him even more.

The barman places another drink in front of each of us.

"Thank you for this. Bottoms up." I chink my glass against the side of his.

"You're very welcome. Bottoms up, Victoria."

I dip my finger into my glass and fish out a raspberry bobbing on the surface, dropping it into my mouth before licking each finger clean. Meanwhile, James's smile never leaves his lips and his gaze narrows as I'm licking my fingers.

"Do you have any plans for later?" he asks.

"Not particularly. We'll see what comes up."

"Comes up," he chortles. "Good one. So I'm assuming at some point you'll want to talk business."

"Oh, must we? Don't you find that *'business',*" I use air-quotes to emphasise the word, "always puts such a dampener on things. And I was just beginning to like you, Just James."

"Indeed, but at some point you'll have to tell me your rates."

"I'm sorry. Rates?" I jerk my head backwards.

"Yes, how much you charge. Based on the conversation we've just had, I'm assuming you and your friend come as a pair. Which, by the way, is fine by me. I couldn't think of a better way to spend my evening than a cosy ménage à trois with you two lovely ladies."

"Oh my God." I stand up and smooth down my Little Black Dress.

"Everything okay?" Mel asks, aware of a change in the energy beside her.

"Time for us to go."

"Okay, but can I finish my drink first?" She drains the contents of her glass.

Just James, realising his faux pas, reaches for my hand. "I'm so sorry, Victoria. I meant no offence. But you have to admit, two stunning girls like yourselves, dressed as you are, perched at the bar in an establishment like this – what was I supposed to assume."

I snatch my hand away. "Don't touch me. And I'll tell you what you could have assumed. Exactly what I said – that we are two friends visiting the city for the weekend. What more could you have gleaned from our conversation?"

"What's going on?" Mel asks, placing her empty glass back down on the counter top.

"This sleaze bag has just asked how much we would charge to sleep with him," I spit, my index finger pointing into Just James's face. If I had any of my drink left, I would chuck the remnants straight into his big smirking mush. I'm expecting Mel to be equally offended, but she throws her head back and belly laughs.

"Oh that's soo funny," she says, picking up her clutch bag and turning to leave, but not before tapping Just James on his chest with the flat of her palm. "Trust me, we appreciate the compliment, but the truth is – you couldn't afford us. Come on, Vicky. Time to go."

"Be careful." He spins on his stool top, watching us leave. "Istanbul can be a dangerous place if you don't know what you're doing."

"No more dangerous than meeting you." I link my arm through Mel's and stomp off in the most elegant, but offended, manner my three-inch heels will allow.

Jumping into a taxi outside the hotel, I turn to Mel, who is still creasing up with laughter beside me. "How can you not be shocked? That guy thought we were prostitutes."

"I know. It's hilarious. Take it as a compliment. To be fair to him, it is unusual to find well dressed, well travelled, cultured and educated young women like our good selves in a place like this... unless we were *a pair of high-class hookers*."

"I suppose. But I've never had anyone proposition me like that before. It was unnerving."

"Me neither. But hey – if we're ever short on cash, at least we know we have a solid future in an alternative career. I bet we could earn a fortune."

"Mel, have you completely lost your senses?" My face cracks into a smile.

"No, of course not, but that's the third time we've been chatted up since leaving Heathrow. I think that's a new record – even for us."

"Well, if Istanbul really is that dangerous, maybe we should just head to the restaurant the guys from the Bazaar gave us the details of. At least we know them, and they saved us loads of money on our shopping."

"And without them we'd never have found the hamman."

"True. I'm not sure I could cope with any more unwelcome surprises tonight."

"Neither am I." She leans forward and gives the taxi driver the new address. Changing lanes on the motorway, he slams his foot to the floor and speeds us towards the city lights.

Chapter 12

We arrive at the address the men gave us. Stepping out of the taxi in front of the restaurant, its front wall pulled back and tables spilling out onto the pavement, we spy the men standing next to a tree – one of many that form a decorative line down the pavement. The taller of them leans back, one leg bent up against the tree trunk, his hands thrust deep inside his pockets. The other faces him, both of them deep in conversation. I fan myself with my clutch bag, the balmy evening air is only marginally cooled by a light breeze that causes the fairy lights festooned around the tree branches to twinkle and dance above our heads.

The taller of the men looks over his cousin's shoulder and spots us stepping out of the taxi. They both stand up straight and watch us glide towards them.

"Ladies! You came."

"Of course we came." Mel air-kisses each man in turn.

I air-kiss Mr Curly-Haired first and before I have a chance to air-kiss Mr Tall, Dark and Handsome's cheek, he bows, reaches for my hand and kisses the back of it, his eyes locked with mine.

"Guzelsin!" he says in Turkish, his white teeth glinting in the moonlight.

"Thank you," I reply, blushing, and he slides a protective hand into the small of my back. Claiming me.

The other man places his hand in the small of Mel's back and they direct us towards a vacant table underneath the nearest tree.

Pulling out my seat for me, Mr Tall, Dark and Handsome asks, "What do you want to drink?"

"Vodka and Coke, please."

After my two Bellinis, I plan to stick to spirits for the rest of the evening. If I switch to wine now, I'll be lolling around like a baboon in a matter of hours.

"I think our night has just got a whole lot better," I grin, leaning forward and whispering to Mel who has taken the seat opposite. "These gentlemen couldn't be more different from the sleaze-bag we left behind at the hotel."

The men order dinner, and before long the table is covered with a variety of meze dishes. I'm not a fan of very spicy food, but somehow the blend of these spices tastes delicious, even to my western palate.

"There is no way we would have found this on our own," Mel whispers.

"I know, we would have ended up in some pricey tourist trap. This is a proper taste of authentic Istanbul."

Over the next few hours, the conversation rolls easily between the four of us. The men try to teach us some basic phrases in Turkish that we attempt to copy with little success, dissolving into fits of giggles as the alcohol takes effect. At no point am I aware of our drinks being topped up, but our glasses are never empty.

At some point a Turkish Rakassa dancer and a trio of players appear on the pavement and circulate among the tables. Her long dark hair flowing down her back as her hips sway from side to side, jangling the coins and beads that hang off her hip scarf and the underside of her bra. She climbs up onto our now cleared table and we all clap and cheer as she twirls her arms in the traditional Romany style. I have no idea whether she is here for our benefit or whether this is a routine she performs every night, but I feel very lucky to be here in this exact moment, experiencing this, even if I'm feeling more than a bit woozy as more alcohol is poured.

She ends her routine with the famous traditional Turkish backbend where she first kneels upright before rolling her shoulders back, arms twisting out in front of her as she continues to lean back, until her shoulders reach the floor behind her, her legs wrapped either side of her body. It's a move I've attempted unsuccessfully in many a yoga class, yet she completes it with ease, her back now flat on the floor.

As the last notes fade on the evening air, we applaud and Mr Tall, Dark and Handsome stands and offers her his hand to help her step down.

Coffees are poured and Mr Tall, Dark and Handsome drapes his arm over the back of my shoulders and strokes the nape of my neck with his thumb. Across the table Mr Curly-Haired does the same to Mel. I can't remember the last time someone paid me such respectful attention and a warm, squidgy feeling settles in the pit of my stomach as his thumb continues to sweep back and forth.

If things continue like this, there's a good chance the evening might end with a cheeky snog under the fairy lights before Mel and I return to the hotel. The perfect way to end a perfect day in this perfect city.

The meal over, somehow the bill is paid. Neither Mel nor I are asked to contribute, nor do we see either of the men settle up.

I'm feeling very, very drunk now and I need Mr Tall, Dark and Handsome to hold me upright as we stand to leave. The guys hail a cab and they bundle us inside. I assume they're about to send us home, but they climb in next to us and I'm too inebriated to object.

I must have fallen asleep against Mr Tall, Dark and Handsome's shoulder as the next thing I'm aware of is half-walking, half-being-carried up a dimly lit staircase and through a door. Could this be some back entrance into our hotel, or the entrance to some exclusive club? My brain is so foggy I can't make sense of what is going on. I am aware that Mel is in an awful state as well, but that she's still there behind me, being half-carried by Mr Curly-Haired.

Once through the door, we're plunged into darkness and I struggle to make out any shapes inside. I flop onto what feels like a couch, or could it be a bed? I can't be sure, and all I want to do is go to sleep. I'm so drunk and incredibly tired. Strangely, I don't feel sick. In the past, if I've ever been this inebriated, I'd have thrown up by now, my body instinctively rejecting the overload of alcohol in my stomach, but everything just feels foggy and I'm struggling to stay conscious.

"May I have a glass of water, please?" I ask Mr Tall, Dark and Handsome as I try to clear the fuzziness in my head and get a handle on our surroundings.

"Of course. I get it for you now," he replies and disappears into the blackness.

I can't see Mel. Where is she? She must be here somewhere. He returns with a drink. I take a sip. It tastes funny, but I drink it anyway.

"Thank you," I slur, my brain struggling to form cohesive sentences. Every blink of my eyelids feels as if they're being pulled down by weights.

He takes my glass and places it on the floor, before turning back towards me and smiling. But this is not the nice warm smile from earlier – this is a lecherous smirk, and a bolt of fear shoots through my body.

I go to get up, but his next move is so fast I have no time to react. He's on top of me before my brain can catch up. His full weight pinning me down flat against the couch beneath me.

"Sen çok güzelsin," he says, his eyes hooded with lust, his features hard with desire.

Leaning forward as if to kiss me, I turn my head away, but he licks the side of my face and my gut contracts in disgust.

"What are you doing?" I scream, still in disbelief at the dramatic change in his demeanour.

"Lie still you silly little girl," he says, pressing his left arm across my windpipe and holding my shoulders down. My arms flapping as I try to push him off me, the fogginess in my brain impedes my coordination and the alcohol in my blood strips me of all my strength.

He reaches under my skirt, hooking one finger into the gusset of my knickers which he yanks sharply, ripping them and pulling them away from my body.

"Noooooo!" I go to scream, but with no air in my lungs, no sound comes out and I flay my arms helplessly. Adrenaline shoots through my body, clearing the fuzziness in my brain just enough for me to comprehend what is happening. Using his free hand, he loosens his belt. Unable to match his strength, I lie flat and stop struggling.

"That's right. Now be a good girl and relax," he hisses.

NO! NEVER! a voice inside my head screams. I'm not going to let this monster take something from me that I can never get back. Not this time. Anger surges through my veins and hones my senses just enough for me to think clearly. Believing I've surrendered, he loosens his grip and shuffles his knees forward, allowing his trousers to drop to his knees. It's all the space I need, and I knee him in the balls as hard as I can. Bullseye!

"GET OFF ME!" I scream, not recognising the sound of my voice.

"Siktir! You bitch!" He rolls off me and onto the floor, clasping his crotch.

I know I have only seconds, so grabbing my bag, and on unsteady legs, I fumble around searching for Mel. "Mel. Me-lan-ie. Where are you?"

Feeling along walls, I push through a door and stumble inside a dimly lit bedroom. Through the darkness I see her, face down, barely conscious and bent forward over a dressing table. Mr Curly-Haired is holding her in place with one hand in the centre of her back. Her dress pulled up, her bare bottom exposed, her knickers long gone and judging by the scene in front of me - he is about to enter her.

"DON'T YOU FUCKING DARE!" I roar, but he ignores me, his eyes remaining focused on the bare flesh in front of him.

However, my scream jolts Mel back from the brink of unconsciousness as her eyes fleetingly focus on me and then on the man behind her. She clenches her hand into a fist and, with one hand over the over, thrusts her elbow backwards, hard, into Mr Curly-Haired's chest. Winded, he stumbles backwards and I run up to him, put both my hands on his shoulders and knee him in the crotch, pulling him forward with as much force as I can command. He falls to his knees, shouting something in Turkish, hugging his exposed genitalia.

I grab Mel and drag her away from him. She reaches back to the dressing table, grappling for her clutch bag.

"Leave it," I shout.

Holding onto each other, we dash for the front door and flee out of the apartment. Our shoes clatter on the concrete stairs. Down one floor, then another, and another. Five flights later, the light of the Ground Floor emergency exit comes into view.

"Almost there." Mel lunges for the panic bar and the door opens instantly as we run for freedom.

Mel is two paces in front and as I reach the doorway, I'm grabbed from behind.

"MEL-AN-IE!" I scream in blind panic as two firm hands drag me kicking and screaming back inside.

It's Mr Tall, Dark and Handsome. He's lifted me off my feet, manhandling me back into the dark stairwell, slamming my face into the hard concrete wall and pinning my arms above my head.

His mouth in my ear, I recoil from his furious breath. "I asked you be a good girl."

His full body weight pressing up behind me, he keeps my arms pressed over my head against the wall, and with his free hand he pulls my skirt up, exposing my naked backside.

Hot, stingy tears burn at the corner of my eyes. I can't escape and I'm powerless to stop him. "MEL-AN-IE," I screech with such force it hurts the back of my throat.

Out of my peripheral vision, I see her charge back in through the fire exit. She leaps onto his back, beating him with her fists like a wild banshee. He lets go of my skirt but keeps my hands pinned above my head, and with his free arm grabs Mel by her hair, smashing her head into the concrete wall beside me. For a split second, we are eye to eye, both of us terrified and unable to break free from his grip.

Trapped and powerless, my vision is drawn to a vertical shaft of light that appears, then widens as a lift door opens on the opposite side of the stairwell. Out steps Mr Curly-Haired and in two clear strides he crosses the stairwell. He grabs Mel and throws her into the opposite corner where she slams against the wall before sliding down and landing in a crumpled heap on the hard floor.

Meanwhile, Mr Tall, Dark and Handsome flips me around, slamming my spine against the concrete behind me. Still keeping my arms pinned above my head, he uses his feet to spread-eagle mine as he fumbles with his belt. His eyes narrow into slits and I close my own, the only defence I have left. Fully expecting the next sensation to be him forcing himself inside me, I hold my breath … and wait.

"Durmak! Yok!"

It's Mr Curly-Haired's voice. I open my eyes. I don't know the meaning of his words, but his tone sounds like an instruction.

"Bırak. Buna değmezler," he says with even more authority this time, and Mr Tall, Dark and Handsome turns his head, listening.

Over the monster's shoulder I make eye contact with Mr Curly-Haired and for the briefest of moments, the world stands still. From the tone of his words, I don't believe he wants to harm me. Rather, the opposite. My heart pounds like a drum inside my chest and blood whooshes through my ears. I lock eyes with Mr Curly-Haired and silently plead for his help.

Raising his voice further, he repeats his previous instruction, placing a hand on Mr Tall, Dark and Handsome's shoulder. "Buna değmezler. Gitmesine izin ver."

Mr Tall, Dark and Handsome releases my arms and takes a small step backwards. I have enough room to escape, but I'm frozen with fear and remain stock still.

Mr Curly-Haired turns and holds out a hand to a winded Mel who is still lying in a crumpled heap on the floor. She takes his hand, and he pulls her unsteadily to her feet. She replaces a missing shoe and smoothes down her skirt.

Reaching a hand behind his back, Mr Curly-Haired retrieves Mel's clutch bag out of the back of his jeans waistband and passes it to her. "Time for you to go."

"With pleasure," Mel says breathlessly. "Come on, Vicky. You heard the man."

I don't need any more time to think, my brain having checked back into gear. I place both my palms on Mr Tall, Dark and Handsome's chest and push him backwards as hard as I can. My last act of defiance.

He laughs, then raises his hand as if to strike me. I wince in preparation for the blow, but instead he turns his hand over and strokes the back of his fingers down my cheek. "Goodbye then, beautiful."

He may not have raped me, but it's clear he wants me to know he could have if he'd wanted to.

"Fuck you," I spit, then before either of them change their minds, Mel and I hold hands and flee out of the open fire door and into the jet-black night sky.

Running away from the building, my breath burns inside my chest. Petrified to look behind me for fear of seeing the men chasing after us again, we have no idea where we are, or how we will get back to our hotel. Looking around, we can see we're in a residential estate filled only with high-rise apartments. The estate seems to be a modern urbanisation, miles away from the lights of the city, its edges surrounded by a black forest, but still we keep running. Turning a corner we spot a yellow ray of hope. A bright yellow cab is parked up, the light showing it's available for hire.

He must have just dropped off a fare. Either that, or it was the same taxi who brought us here, and he has been asked to wait, or has hung around, perhaps aware of what was about to happen to the two half-conscious western girls who were being transported away from the city centre by some locals.

We don't care and jump inside, giving the driver the name of our hotel before he speeds off into the night, taking us back to safety.

"The bastard," Mel says, while I stare blankly out of the side window.

"What?" I ask, turning to look at her, hoping she doesn't want to talk about what's just happened. I'm nowhere near ready to pick over this evening's events.

"He stole all my money." She snaps her purse shut and tosses it between us on the back seat.

"All things considered Mel, I think that's the best possible outcome we could have hoped for from tonight," I whisper, before turning back to stare numbly out of the window again.

Part Four

Chapter 13

"Eurgh," Mel groans the next morning, a cool damp cloth draped across her forehead. "I wish someone would switch off the jackhammer inside my head." She covers her eyes with her hand.

As well as severe headaches, we're both covered in bruises. My shoulders, my hip bones and my right cheek clearly don't agree with being slammed into a hard concrete wall. Even my wrists and collarbones bear the evidence of being forcibly pinned. Mel has a shiner of a black eye and no skin on her knees where she landed on the stairwell floor.

From underneath my damp facecloth, I mumble, "I wasn't sure we'd make it out alive, Mel."

"No shit, Sherlock. It was bloody terrifying."

We both pause, and I know she too is reflecting on all the horrific 'what ifs'.

"How come we were so wasted?" I say. "I know we've both been blind drunk before, but one of us is usually compos mentis enough to get the other home before any harm's done. One minute we were enjoying dinner; I remember the belly dancer on the table, but everything after that is fuzzy."

"I think they drugged us. It's the only explanation."

The strange taste of the water Mr Tall, Dark and Handsome gave me at the flat comes rushing back. He must have been lacing my drinks all evening. My mouth fills with saliva as if trying to cleanse my palate all over again.

"When I think about it now," Mel continues, "they drank bottled beer all night, whereas they plied us with vodka, which they must have laced with gawd knows what."

"That would explain our blinding headaches. I've never had a hangover this bad before." I pause before adding, "Should we report them to the police?"

"What would be the point? Who'd believe us? After the restaurant we don't know where they took us, and even if they were arrested they're bound to say we went of our own free will. It would be their word against ours."

"Even with these bruises?"

"We fly home in a few hours, Vicky. If we stay and make statements we'd miss our flight, and do *you* want to come back and have to face them in court, because I sure as hell don't." She reaches across the void between our beds and clasps my hand. "We're okay, aren't we? I agree, it could have been a lot worse, but we escaped and in the end there was no harm done – not really."

"Maybe. But it still feels wrong that they can do what they did and get away with it. What if the next two women are not as lucky?"

"Let it go, Vicky. Life goes on, and the best thing we can do is forget the whole hideous episode."

"I think you're right. I don't think I could get out of bed to go to the police even if I wanted to."

"In hindsight, maybe a ménage à trois with the guy from the bar would have been the safer option." She rolls her eyes.

"Oh, don't make me laugh. Everything hurts."

"At least we'd have got paid." She laughs in return, before gripping her forehead in pain.

. . .

On the flight home, and after pushing the tasteless food around the plastic airline tray, I turn and gaze out of the window. The lights of Istanbul are long gone and the sky outside is a dark blue hue with a strip of orange as the sun slips below the horizon.

What the hell is wrong with me? Why do I always seem to attract the worst possible men? Men that want nothing more than to violate and abuse me. Last night was not the first time I've ended up in an unsafe situation where a member of the opposite sex has exploited me. And in both cases, the men involved have got away with it.

Last night I escaped, but the previous time I wasn't so lucky. Instead, my only defence became my unwillingness to participate once he had overpowered me. I discovered I could retreat into myself and disconnect my mind from my body. The naiveté of my inexperience and the embarrassment of what I'd allowed to happen shaming me into a lifetime of silence. Perhaps it was my fault? Maybe I gave him the wrong impression, and I harbour so much guilt for not fighting back.

This morning would have been the perfect opportunity to have shared my hideous secret with Mel, but what if, appreciating I'd had something similar happen before, she blamed me for what happened last night? Expecting me to have been more cautious. To have had enough sense for the both of us.

It happened four years ago, during my first term of college. It had started out like any other normal night after lectures had finished. I could hardly hear myself think over the blare of the music inside the Student Union bar. The makeshift dance floor, in the middle of room, inviting a bunch of half-cut students to 'vogue' along with Madonna's latest single.

My friends and I had nabbed a long table by the windows. Each side set with wooden benches that lined up in one continuous line, like one long school dinner table. Our student bar was within the campus of our Halls of Residence, so it wasn't massive, not like the main uni bar down in the centre of town. Rather, this drinking hole felt more like a cosy local pub. A place you could walk into on your own and be confident you'd bump into at least one person you knew. Myself and my group of friends had got into the habit of going there every day after lectures, intending to sup one beer, before we'd head back to our dorms to study, or cook, or hang out in each other's rooms. But, like many evenings, that plan had gone by the wayside once the bar filled up and the evening progressed.

"What's your poison?" I remember the deep reverberation of his voice.

I'd turned away from the conversation buzzing between my girlfriends on the other side of the table and looked at the stranger who'd slid himself onto the bench next to me. "Sorry? Were you talking to me?"

He'd flashed me a kilowatt smile and held out his hand. "Pete. Nice to meet you. And you are?"

"Victoria." I'd shaken his hand and felt my lips pulling into an unconscious smile.

"Is this your halls?" he'd asked.

"Yes."

"Do you always drink here? Or do you ever venture further afield?"

"A bit of both. We come in here most nights and sometimes head elsewhere at the weekends. But I don't think I've seen you here before?"

"No. A bunch of us thought we'd give one of the other college bars a look." He'd scanned the room. "Looks like a decent crowd though."

"It is."

There was a pause, while neither of us said anything, then he'd pointed at my empty glass and asked again, "What's your poison? I'm heading to the bar. Let me buy you a drink."

"Vodka and Coke, please. Are you sure ... you don't mind?"

"Not at all. A pretty girl like you should never have an empty glass."

I'd dipped my chin and hoped he couldn't see the flush creeping up my neck. It was almost the end of my first term at college, and this stranger was the first guy who'd paid me any attention – at least in that way. I had male friends, for sure. But having all met at Fresher's Week, all my new friends, both boys and girls, had paired off, leaving me the only singleton in our fragile friendship group.

"Back in a bit." He'd swung his leg over the bench and disappeared into the smokey crowd.

One of my girlfriends had leaned across the wooden table. "Oi oi. Someone's gone all red."

Placing my hands over my cheeks, I'd replied, "Stop it. You're making me blush. He's only buying me a drink."

If only I'd known then what would happen later, I would have fled the bar before he'd reappeared, but moments later he returned. Two drinks in tow.

All evening I'd lapped up his compliments like a starving dog, believing he was genuinely interested in me and this could be the start of something amazing. Don't most people meet their future husbands at university?

We'd spent the whole evening engrossed in conversation, oblivious to the surrounding activity. His smokey grey eyes had remained locked onto mine and the rest of the world fell away. The crowd in the bar a hazy smudge around us. The beat from the jukebox muted to a soft muffle, his voice cutting through all the noise like a knife through butter. His kind, open face had laughed at everything I'd said and I remember the electric shock of his fingers when he'd leaned forward and placed a hand on my knee. When he'd tucked a loose tendril of hair behind my ear, I'd instinctively dipped my head into his palm.

Of course I'd allowed him to walk me back across the quadrant to my dorm, when I'd said I needed to get back and finish an assignment for the next day. I was expecting him to ask to see me again and seal his promise with a first kiss. But what came next happened so fast it still shocks me to think about it. I can't remember how he forced his way into my room, locked the door and kept me prisoner. After my attempts to escape, fight back or appeal to his humanity all failed, and my shouts for help went unanswered – my friends all still down in the bar – I discovered that by detaching my mind from my body, I could protect my soul. He could penetrate my body, but never my heart.

The events of last night in Istanbul may have paled in comparison to the horror of that dark night at college, but how could I have been so stupid – again? There must have been clues. If not, how the hell am I supposed to know when a man is ever genuine?

This past weekend the Turkish Airlines Pilots, Just James and Mr Tall, Dark and Handsome all seemed perfectly charming. But they all lied to cover their true motivations. To them, I am nothing more than an available vagina.

I only ever seem to meet three types of men: those I fall for, like Mr Summer-Fling or Mr STI, who reject my affections or betray my trust after I've opened my heart to them; men like the rapist from college or the locals from last night, who appear genuine and charming but whose intentions are self-motivated and who will go to any lengths to have their physical needs met; or safe but unexciting men like Steve. He may have been a lazy slob, but he never once raised his hand or forced himself on me. Perhaps men like him, less powerful or attractive men, are the safer option?

I reach across the armrest of my airline seat and interlock my fingers with Mel's. United in our shared experience. She squeezes my hand as we smile weakly at each other.

"Well, Istanbul has been nothing if not eventful," Mel says, raising her eyebrows.

"I'll never forget it," I reply, blinking away my tears.

Chapter 14

Back at work the following week, and covered with panstick makeup to hide our bruises, Mel and I spend the next few days buried in complex travel requests. We simply relay tales of the hustle and bustle of the Grand Bazaar or the tranquillity of the hamman and leave out any further details of our trip, if any of the company PAs ask us about our most recent jaunt away.

My phone rings and, keeping my eyes on my computer screen, I cradle the handset under my chin. "Travel Bureau. Victoria speaking."

"Hi Victoria, there's a package for you in reception," the lady on the front desk announces.

"Oh? We don't have any deliveries booked in for today. Does it seem valuable?" Placing my palm over the mouthpiece I whisper to Mel, "You're not waiting for a rush visa, or any special currency are you?"

She shakes her head. "Could you send it down to the post room, please? I'll swing by later and collect it."

"Ahem, I think you need to come and collect this one in person, Victoria."

"Err, okay. I'm on my way." Replacing the handset, I swivel my chair in Mel's direction and shrug.

"Best go find out," she says.

I round the corner into the atrium and the spring sunshine streams in through the glass roof, while a pungent aroma assaults the inside of my nose. The receptionist's desk is obliterated by a massive bouquet of hand-tied roses. The blood-red blooms accentuated by sprigs of white gypsum and green foliage.

"Someone's popular," the receptionist says, passing me the bouquet.

Blushing, I rush back down the corridor, my eyes only just peeking through the bouquet. No one has ever sent me flowers to my workplace before. In fact, I can count on a few fingers how many times I've ever been sent flowers. Once by Mr STI after a particularly nice date, but they were sent to my parents' address, not my workplace, and the only other time was an Interflora bouquet that turned up at Steve's. At the time my heart had done a little flip inside my chest, thinking they might have been from him, but it turned out to be a gift from an aunt for my birthday.

As I'm walking back into our office, Mel lifts her nose out of an International Travel Directory. "Jeez, who are they from?"

"No bloody idea." I plonk the flowers on my desk and rip the envelope from the top right-hand corner of the cellophane.

My mind flicks through all the possibilities. Could they be from my mum? Maybe if they were carnations or a mixed bouquet, but not roses. What about the jerks from Istanbul? We had told them where we worked. Maybe they want to apologise. But I doubt it. Not after what they did, including robbing Mel. So who else?

Opening the envelope, my heart sinks when I read the name at the bottom of the printed card. I pass it to Mel and she reads aloud, "These past four months have been the worst of my life. I love you. Please come home. Steve. Kiss, kiss, kiss."

She hands the card back to me and I flop down in my chair. Dropping my head into my hands, I'm unable to stop the river of tears that erupt from the corners of my eyes. It's all just too much. Istanbul. The memories from college. And now Steve.

"Hey, hey." Mel is beside me, rubbing my knee. "Don't cry, Chook. It's not that bad."

"Oh, but it is," I wail. "Why does everything to do with the opposite sex have to be so damn hard? Why can't I just find someone *nice?* Someone fun, but someone who would look after me. Someone to just *be* with. Michelle's found David. All my friends back home are coupled up. Why am I the only one all alone?"

"Err, hello. Remember me? I'm single but I don't feel '*alone*'."

"But I do, and I don't like it. My love life scores a crappy 'U' for Undesirable."

"It's true that you have had a pretty shitty run of late, but I wouldn't go that far. I'd score you more a 'D' – tries hard but hasn't yet reached their full potential." She smiles and my spirits lift a smidgeon. I can always count on Mel to lighten my mood. Yet, there's one massive difference between us. Mel, I've learnt, thrives as a singleton, whereas I hate being unattached. Being single doesn't worry Mel, whereas I want to make it as short a temporary situation as possible. A malady to be swiftly remedied at the first available opportunity.

More serious now, I say what I'm thinking. "Maybe I've made a terrible mistake, Mel. Maybe I shouldn't have been so harsh on Steve and so quick to throw the towel in. I know he could be a bit of a slob, but he cared about me, and this proves he misses me and wants me back."

"But you were miserable living with him."

"Maybe. But what if the next guy I meet turns out just the same as the sleazebags in Istanbul, or like that guy, James, from the bar? Or the pilots." I don't add, and the one you don't know about from college. I turn the card over and over in my hand and study the note. "How are you ever meant to know who's genuine and who's not? I think I'll call him."

"Oh don't, Chook. I know this past weekend was awful, but going back to Steve's not the answer."

But before we're able to continue the conversation, our phones ring simultaneously. Placing the roses on the floor behind my desk and snapping back into work mode, I pick up my telephone as Mel does the same. I'm noting down the details of another travel request, while Mel, with both hands cupped around her handset, focuses her eyes on me. Waiting until I replace my handset, she says to the caller, "She's free now. I'll pop you through." Turning to me, she mouths, *'It's your mum.'*

"Hi Mam," I say cheerily when the call clicks through.

"Hi Poppet." She sounds strained.

"What's up?"

"I have some bad news, sweetheart."

"Oh? What's up?" She bursts into tears and a cold fear shrouds over me. "Mam, don't cry. What on earth's the matter?" I ask, but she's unable to speak. The sound of her crushing sobs blur into the background as she steps away from the phone. "Mam. What's happened? Tell me?" I shout into the void.

"Victoria?" My stepdad picks up the handset.

"Yes?"

"It's not good news, I'm afraid. Grandad has taken a turn for the worse. He was rushed into hospital a few hours ago and they don't think he'll make it through the night. I suggest you get yourself home – and fast."

I suck in a sharp breath and clamp my hand over my mouth. My grandfather has not been in the best of health for a few years, so although this news is not a complete shock, this is the call I never wanted to receive.

"Victoria? Are you still there?" he asks when I go silent.

"Yes. I'm still here," I reply, one hand flying across my keyboard, booking the next scheduled flight to Newcastle. "I'm on my way. I'll call you from Heathrow."

We sign off, and while I wait for my ticket to run through our office printer, I wrap my fingers around my grandad's precious Masonic Orb that hangs around my neck. The gift he gave me for my twenty-first birthday. Fashioned into a necklace, it's my most precious possession. Hang in there Grandad. Hang on until I get there – please.

Walking through the screen doors at Newcastle Airport four hours later and looking into my mother's eyes, I know I'm too late. My darling, funny, generous grandfather has gone forever. Without a father growing up (my mother only remarried when I was fifteen) my grandad was my primary paternal influence and I adored him. But now I'll never see him again. Never hear him giggle at his own jokes. Never feel the weight of his arms wrapped around me, keeping me safe. Never see the joy on his face when I would run into his lap.

No parent, or grandparent, should have favourites, but unlike the rest of my cousins, who all had neat, complete families, my mother landed back home in a heap after the collapse of her marriage to my father, and my grandparents nurtured us both back to stability and health. My earliest memories of *'home'* were under my granny and grandad's roof.

Theirs was a house that ran like clockwork, on account of my grandmother's background in Service, and woe betide anyone who upset the smooth running of her ship. Monday was always wash day, Tuesdays she spent ironing and doing housework. Wednesdays we would find her tending her vegetable patch and gardening. Thursday mornings she always went to town to get her hair done, followed by trips to the butchers and greengrocer's, but Fridays were always my favourite. Friday was baking day and she would leave bowl after bowl of cake mix for me to lick out. Long into my childhood, I would rush in from school on a Friday night and, armed with a wooden spatula, dig in with gusto until all the mixing bowls were squeaky clean.

But in-between the formalities of set meal times and her army-like routine, just like sweet jam between the layers of one of her Victoria Sponges, my grandparents' house was always filled with love. Even now, I often dream of being back there. The recurring vision appearing whenever my life seems out of kilter. In the dream, I'm a child again, sitting at the top of the stairs, looking down into the empty hallway below. With my knees tucked under my chin and my nightie pulled down round my ankles, keeping me warm, I can hear Granny humming to herself while she cleans the hearth and lights the fire in the front room. Meanwhile, the smell of home-baked apple pie, or other such comforting goodies would swirl through the house.

If I cock my head, I hear the click of the back door latch as Grandad arrives home for breakfast, having risen at dawn and already done a couple of hours' work. The rustle of him stripping out of his bib and brace overtrousers, hanging them along with his flat cap on his peg by the back door, before he steps into the kitchen. *'Hellooo. Anyone home?'* he hollers before settling into his chair at the head of the table and pouring himself a cup of tea from the cosy-covered pot that was a permanent fixture in the middle of the kitchen table. In the dream, I may be at the top of the stairs, only listening and observing rather than participating in the world below, but I always wake feeling warm, loved, and most of all – safe.

I sense my vision will return tonight.

Collapsing into my mother's open arms, she strokes my hair as grief rips through me, as visceral as if someone had ripped a limb from my body.

"Oh, I'm so sorry, Victoria. At least he didn't suffer. He would have hated it if he'd been left to rot for years and years."

"But I wanted to see him," I sob. "To say goodbye."

"I know, darling. But he wouldn't have known you were there, even if you had made it in time. He was already slipping away."

"But I would have known."

"I know, sweetheart. I know."

Chapter 15

The next few days pass in a snot-filled, red-eyed blur, as my extended family grieve the loss of our beloved patriarch. My grandfather was in every sense the head of our family, and now that he's gone, we're all feeling the gaping wound left by his death. We take it in turns to rally round Granny, although, out of everyone, our stoic grandmother seems to be taking the loss of her husband in her stride. Born into a generation expected to maintain a stiff upper lip no matter what, she may be grieving in private, but in public she remains resigned but buoyant.

I return to work the following Monday, before flying north again for the funeral later that week. Following behind the hearse in one of the official funeral cars, I'm not surprised hundreds of people are lining the streets around our village church, the pews inside already packed with mourners. My grandfather was a prominent member of our community. A man who forged his own fortune through spit, grit, and determination, but who gave back to others along the way.

The wake is held at my grandparent's sprawling Edwardian home, and I stay behind to help clear up, staking my position at the kitchen sink. I know every nook and cranny of this house and its two-acre garden. Even after my mother and I moved out, once she'd put her life back together, I've spent many a school holiday playing in solitude in its rambling grounds. At least I had a vivid imagination to keep myself occupied.

"Now then Missy." Granny bustles up behind me, carrying another armful of empty plates. "How are you doing? What with everything that's been going on, we've not had a chance to catch up. Not properly. So tell me, what's going on with you?"

"Oh, you know, Granny. Just work mainly, and the gym."

"Well, don't lose any more weight. You're far too skinny for my liking as it is." She pats my arm, before grabbing a tea towel and picking up a wet plate from the draining board. "If you still lived here, I'd be fattening you up. In fact, why don't you stay over tonight? Your room's always made up. And it's baking day tomorrow." She winks.

"I'd love to stay over." We exchange a smile as I pass her another plate to dry.

"And I hope you're not working too hard at that fancy job of yours. What is it they say? *All work and no play makes Jack a dull boy.*"

"I try not to, Granny. I love my job and it can be stressful, but I have fun as well. You remember my housemate, Mel?" She nods. "We went to Istanbul for the weekend not long back."

"Now that's a bit more interesting. I'm such an old relic I can remember when it was still called Constantinople." She chuckles. "I went there with your grandfather, you know."

"Did you? I never knew that. When?"

"Back in the fifties. It was the year after he sold the business and we cruised around the world on the QEII. We called into Istanbul before sailing on to Alexandria, then through the Suez Canal and on to Kenya. Interesting place, but full of savages as I remember."

An involuntary shiver ripples down my spine. "It *was* interesting. Lots of culture and exotic smells. We had a good mooch around, followed by a lovely relaxing afternoon in a hamman."

"Only men could do that type of thing when I was there. All the ladies from the ship weren't allowed to go anywhere without a chaperone. I remember being stared at as we walked around. It was as if they'd never seen women before."

I don't share with Granny, but I remember that same feeling. Strangers' eyes trailing Mel and I as we browsed the stalls of the Grand Bazaar. If only we'd realised then what was to come.

"Thankfully, the hamman was women only," I continue. "Or at least there were only women there when we went. Just as well, as we had to strip down to our birthday suits."

"Oh my goodness. I wouldn't have liked that."

Even when I lived under Granny's roof, I'd only ever seen her fully dressed in her everyday uniform of sensible shoes, wool stockings, a cotton housedress always worn with a matronly pinny over the top to protect it from any spills. She wouldn't be seen dead downstairs in her dressing gown.

"And have you found yourself a nice young man yet? You're not getting any younger you know. You don't want to leave it too late."

I busy myself scrubbing a greasy platter. "Not yet, Granny. Still working on it."

"I really liked the last one. Steve. Wasn't that his name? Such a shame things didn't work out there. I thought he'd be the one to slide a ring on your finger."

My shoulders stiffen. For all our problems, Steve charmed the pants off my family, and if I'd let him I'd likely by engaged by now. It's two weeks since he sent me the bouquet of roses and I had planned to call him that afternoon, but then my mother rang and with everything that's happened since, I haven't had a chance.

"You're the last of my grandchildren to settle down, you know. And now that your grandad's gone..." she sniffs, "I won't rest until you've found yourself a nice young man to look after you."

"I have been trying."

"By your age, I was married with my second bairn on the way."

"What? At twenty-three?"

"Oh yes. In my day, you were *on the shelf* if you weren't married by twenty-one. You were an old maid if you were single and childless by your age, and no one wanted that."

"But you were lucky to find Grandad when you did. All the men I seem to meet are liars, bone idle, or downright sleazebags. I wish I knew where I was going wrong."

One of my cousins walks into the kitchen carrying another stack of empty plates. "I think that's the last of them," she says, one hand affectionately stroking her pregnant belly before she disappears back into the hum-drum of the front room.

"Ah, but that's where you're wrong," Granny continues. "It wasn't luck, we made it work. I met your grandad at the local dance when we were eighteen. He asked me out to the flicks the following week. Then we went out for ice-cream and two months later we were engaged. You kids today. You want it all. Maybe your standards are too high, Missy. I blame the pill."

"Granny!"

"Well, it's true. We never worried about all that stuff. If you went steady with someone, you got married. It was that simple. We didn't have the same aspirations or expectations all you young people have today. You want a career *and* a family. You want to earn your own money *and* have a husband to take care of you. No wonder you haven't found the right man yet, Victoria. Your generation has set the bar impossibly high. Men don't know what's expected of them anymore. The world's turned upside down and the lines are all blurred." She pats the back of my rubber-gloved hand. "But listen to me rambling on. When I met your grandad, I was happy knowing we were fond of each other, and our love grew over a lifetime of mutual respect and shared experiences. Back then, you just hoped you'd picked someone with a mild temperament who wouldn't raise their hand to you or steal the housekeeping and spend it on drink. It wasn't complicated. You young 'uns have muddled everything up."

"I am trying, Granny. I promise. Nothing would make me happier than to settle down. It's exhausting being single and constantly trying to find Mr Right." I turn and look at her, blinking away the tears in my eyes. "I'm terrified I'll end up – as you would say – an old maid."

"Oh, Missy." She pulls me into a hug. "Don't you worry. I'm sure he's out there. Probably right under your nose. Just pick someone kind who won't steal the housekeeping and you'll soon see how happy you can be."

Letting out a deep sigh, I wipe my eyes dry, and think about everything she's just said.

Chapter 16

The following Tuesday evening, with my granny's words still rattling around my head, I'm sitting opposite Steve in Sally Pussey's Inn, a small country pub on the outskirts of Swindon.

"I can't tell you how happy I am to see you," he gushes. A smile splitting his face in two while I stare blankly into my glass of wine.

He's lost weight, giving his jaw a sharper line, and his unruly mop top of mad curls has had a stylish trim. Instead of his usual plaid shirts and brown cords with worn knees and saggy crotch, he's wearing a smart pair of Levi's and a blue Ralph Lauren shirt with noticeable creases ironed down each arm. Lying on the seat next to him is a new navy Berghaus Gortex wind beater, and instead of his tired old muddy hiking boots, his feet are encased in a mustard-coloured pair of suede Timberlands.

"Thank you for coming," he says, his voice wobbling. "When I didn't hear from you, I thought that was it. Game over." He places one hand on the table, palm up, inviting me to slide my hand inside his, but when I don't – preferring to keep my fingers wrapped around the stem of my glass – he retracts it and sucks in a deep breath. His eyes glance around the pub as if looking for the emergency exits.

"I appreciated the flowers, Steve. That was very thoughtful, but it's been a stressful time, what with Grandad dying ..."

"Yes, yes, of course. I understand. I only wished you'd called so I could have been there for you. Come home with you. It's not as if I don't know your family, or they wouldn't have been pleased to see me."

I stay silent, staring into my wine.

'I'm not promising anything,' I'd said when I'd made the call the evening after I'd arrived back in the south after the funeral.

'Me neither,' he'd replied. *'But I'd love to see you … to talk.'*

Mel was furious.

'Have you taken leave of your senses? You were the one who told me he didn't want a girlfriend, he needed a housekeeper. Someone to cook and clean up after him.'

'Maybe,' I'd defended, my tone more elevated than I'd intended. *'But I'm not brave like you. I haven't travelled the world with only a rucksack on my back, not worrying about where I'm going to sleep that night. The bravest thing I've ever done was moving south, to be with Steve. And that was monumental. I'm not sure I have it in me to keep searching for 'the one'. Maybe he is my person after all, and I haven't even thanked him for the flowers. The least I should do is hear what he has to say.'*

'I'm not so sure. But hey, it's your life.'

I look across the table and give Steve a meek smile.

"I don't know about you, but I've been miserable since you left," he continues, spurred on by my tentative encouragement. "I can't lie. I was angry, furious actually, when you walked out without warning, and I spent the next few weeks trying to push you out of my mind." He looks at me and his large brown irises dilate. "But my love for you has refused to die."

I give him my hand to hold and he clasps it like a baby baboon clinging to its mother. "I'm sorry I hurt you. That was never my intention," I say. "I promise you I wasn't thinking about leaving until the day I left. But when I came into the kitchen that morning and saw the mess, I just snapped. But that doesn't mean there wasn't a time I didn't love you."

"I know. I always knew you loved me. Love me still." He takes his hand back and clears his throat. "I've been waiting to see you again, so I can give you this. And now seems as good a time as any."

He pulls a small black velvet box from the inside pocket of his wind beater and slides it across the table. Adrenalin flashes through my veins and my heart rate spikes. He opens the box and a tiny solitaire diamond set in a slim gold band glints back at me.

"Victoria. I want you back. And I want you to know … I forgive you … for leaving."

I jerk my head back.

"I'll hold nothing you said or did against you. All I want is for you to come home – forever. I want us to wipe the slate clean and start over – as a married couple."

My hackles raised, my eyes narrow. "And let's just say I come back, and we get married. What would be different?"

He throws his head back and lets out a throaty laugh. "I get it – trick question, right? Nothing would change, my darling. We would carry on right where we left off."

"Right."

"Isn't that what you want? To go back to how things were, when everything was perfect? Surely now you've had a few months to reflect, you've realised what a good thing we had going. Why else would you have come along tonight? I believe you're here because you've been waiting for me to do this." He gestures towards the box, lying like a landmine on the table between us, and signals for me to pick it up and inspect the tiny diamond.

I take a long, slow sip of my wine, while strategically avoiding Steve's questioning stare and resisting his encouragement to inspect the contents of the box.

My mind drifts back to some happier times during our two years together. The quiet moments curled up in front of the fire, watching the flames dance and crackle in the grate. Or snuggled up together watching a movie and sharing a bottle of wine on a dark winter's night. Or after an intense week at work, trailing through spring meadows of bluebells, or trudging across rolling farmland on one of the many countryside trails on his doorstep. After the craziness of more recent times living with Mel, part of me hankers back to the steady monotony of the life I shared with the man in front of me now.

But as proposals go, Steve's attempt is hardly a romantic fairy tale. He hasn't actually asked me the fateful question. It's as if he's testing me out before he drops to one knee in case I humiliate him. And what about his inability to acknowledge that anything was ever wrong between us? If I go back, any flaws in our relationship will be mine alone to own. Forever.

I'm standing at a crossroads, but which route should I take?

If only I could resummon the police officer from the lay-by that day. Ask him to dial into his control room and get them to give the precise coordinates of the next destination on my life map.

Perhaps I should heed my grandmother's advice and be realistic about my expectations, and accept Steve for who he is and the life he is offering me. Life, after all, isn't made up of sparkling unicorns and princesses being rescued by charming princes. As Granny pointed out only days ago, a long marriage is built on fondness, mutual respect, and a life of shared experiences.

Or should I take a leaf out of Mel's book and let Steve go, and hope there is someone better out there? Someone who has more spunk, who won't abuse me and, instead, keep me safe. Someone who will expand my horizons and take me places I've never been, figuratively and literally.

"You're making me nervous, darling. I'm serious, Victoria. I love you and want you home."

"I know, but do you want *me* to come home? Or do you just want me *home*?"

"I'm not sure I understand. What's the difference?"

"And therein lies the problem." I pinch the bridge of my nose.

There's no doubt a life with Steve would be the safer option, but would it kill my spirit? Deep down, there is a little bubble of energy inside of me waiting to get out. I felt it in the afterglow of the amazing massage in the hamman. I even felt it when I refused to surrender and fought back against my capture in Istanbul. It's there. A spirit fizzing away in my gut, waiting for me to find the right outlet through which to express it. To find the person who will release that part of me and let it soar. That's what I've been searching for – the conduit through which to experience my best life. And with absolute certainty, I've just realised, Steve is not it. He doesn't want *me,* as much as he thinks he does, he just wants someone – anyone – to look after him.

Hurriedly, I gather up my things. "I'm sorry. I shouldn't have come. This was a mistake."

Steve lunges for my hand. "Wait," he half-laughs. "Don't leave. Sit down. Finish your drink. Let us talk about this like adults. I want to talk about our future." Still holding my hand, he slides off the chair and onto one knee.

I hear a couple of pub patrons gasp and one woman digs her partner in the ribs and points over in our direction. I squeeze my eyes shut, but I'm too slow to stop him.

"Victoria Turnbull. I love you with my whole heart. Will you marry me?" he blurts out.

Everyone in the pub holds their breath.

Holding my head high and pushing my shoulders back, I keep my voice steady and firm. "Steve, I'm sorry, but this *was* a mistake. Maybe I came because I felt I owed you the chance to explain yourself. Maybe I was curious. Maybe I hoped you'd changed, but I see now that if I came back things may be good for a short time, but the life you want isn't the life I want. Since I left, I've been moving forwards, not backwards. Sure, I've made some mistakes and I've been sad that things didn't work out between us, and there are parts of our life together that I do miss. But if I came back now, nothing would change. I've just got my life started, and I don't want to unstart it. If I came back now, that's what it would feel like – a life unstarted. And that wouldn't be fair on either of us. I know you think you want me, but really – you need a housekeeper, not a wife."

"But you're wrong." He subtly slides back onto his chair, still clasping my hand, realising that once he lets go, that final tentative thread between us will be broken. "Since you've been gone, I've turned over a new leaf. Just this morning I spilt orange juice on the counter, and in the past I wouldn't have noticed and would have left it to go all sticky, but I didn't. I wiped it up."

I swallow hard. "Steve. I appreciate you inviting me tonight, I really do. But this is my life, and my decision. You may have learnt to clean up after yourself, but that's not the point. I want something you can't give me."

He releases my hand and whispers, "Well, I hope you find what you're looking for."

"So do I." I push my chair back and stand up. "Goodbye, Steve. Good luck."

I head towards the door. Out of the corner of my eye I spy him draining his pint, leaving beer foam down the inside of the glass, before he stretches one hand across the table to retrieve the small black box, sliding it back inside the pocket of his wind beater. He glances around the room, assessing how many people witnessed his rejection, but they give him the privacy of anonymity by politely ignoring him.

Outside, the fresh spring air hits me as if I were a convict newly released from jail. My hand over my chest, I suck in a couple of cleansing breaths. Skipping down the pavement, I head back towards Mel. Back towards an unknown future. Back towards a world of possibility.

Looking around as the spring sunshine renews the earth, the hedgerows bursting with fresh green shoots, the grass verges covered in a carpet of yellow daffodils, I angle my cheek towards the sun. Feeling the gentle evening rays warm my skin, I remember the words I muttered to myself the first time I left Steve: *'Okay, universe. I have no idea what I'm doing or where I'm headed, so if you have a plan for me – it would be really helpful if you could give me a hint sometime soon.'*

I still may not know what the future holds for me. Who knows, maybe I'll never find that special someone, but right now, just knowing I have that possibility is enough.

Two Saturdays later, Mel and I are up in London, partying at Tim's swanky Surrey Quays pad, the moody black Thames snaking silently past outside. Fuelled by alcohol and high-spirits, someone suggested we move the party downstairs and into the apartment's communal swimming pool.

Mel and I change into our swimming costumes and, emerging first from the Ladies' changing rooms, Mel dives in. Swimming underwater, she heads towards Tim who is standing amongst a group of colleagues in the middle of the pool. She reaches up and rips down the back of his trunks, revealing his lily white bottom.

"Oi you cheeky minx," he laughs, splashing her and starting a play-fight.

Meanwhile, I notice a pair of piercing blue eyes looking out at me from the water, following my form as I head towards the steps. A powerful arm reaches up, offering me a steady hand as I glide into the pool.

"Here, let me help you," Jeremy says.

"Thank you," I reply graciously, taking the hand that's offered.

"I was hoping you'd be here tonight." He beams, using his free hand to run his fingers through his blonde locks, flipping his floppy fringe back into place.

"Me too," I say, smiling as I float into the water next to him. If nothing else, tonight has shown me never know what may be lying around the next corner, just waiting for the planets to collide.

Epilogue

CHRIS

Christchurch, New Zealand, The same day

Chris turns and looks out of the passenger window at the rust, red, and amber leaves on the trees. A shiver ripples through his body. Autumn has well and truly arrived, but he doesn't mind the chill in the air today. In a matter of hours, he'll be soaking up the thirty-degree heat, stretched out on a white sandy beach, beer in hand.

"Not long now," Chris's dad says. "What's your plan once you land in Bangkok?"

"Oh, you know me, Dad. Make it up as I go along. I've got five weeks to chill before I head to London. I'll probably jump on whichever is the first flight down to the islands. I don't mind whether it's Koh Samui or Phuket."

"Well, you know them all. Looking forward to it?"

"Definitely."

"And when you get to England, give my daughters a big hug from me."

"I will. I'm looking forward to seeing them. Although I can't say I've missed Mich bossing me around, but it'll be great to hang out with Mellie. Three years is too long."

"You two were always so close growing up." Chris's dad yanks on the handbrake as he reaches the drop-off zone at Christchurch International Airport. "When do you think you'll be back?"

Chris shrugs, climbing out onto the pavement. "When it starts to get cold over there, or my money runs out. Whichever comes first."

"Count yourself lucky, son. I know lots of people who would love the freedom to take off as frequently as you do."

"And that's why I'll always be self-employed, Dad. You know that."

"Well, I'm proud of you. It's not like you had the easiest of childhoods, what with your eye and everything, but you've never let it stop you going after what you want."

Chris's dad shuffles from foot to foot on the pavement next to the car as Chris pulls his pack from the boot. "Have a good time, son," he says, slapping Chris on the back. "Don't do anything I wouldn't do."

"Really, Dad? That's your best bit of advice? The man from the Navy telling me to behave myself."

Chris's father is the original Pom of the family, who after a long career, first in the British Navy followed by the Merchant Navy, settled in New Zealand when he met and married Chris's mother. Twenty years and four kids later, he decided she wasn't the one for him and blew everyone's lives apart when he ran away with his best friend's wife. Chris's mum was heartbroken. Wedded before God, according to her strong Catholic beliefs, is an unbreakable vow. Another decade on and Chris's father seems settled in his second marriage, even if the family's scars remain.

"Right now, I'm only thinking about chillin' on a beach, before catching up with my rellies when I get to England, then tramping around Europe for the rest of the summer," Chris continues.

"Well, don't go falling for any English Roses while you're over there. If any more of my children migrate back to the Mother Country, I may just have to re-migrate back there myself. And I can't stand the weather. Just remember, Christopher, it rains all the time, and I mean … all the bloody time!"

"First sign of rain and I'll be on a plane to Greece. It's top of my list. Trust me, I've no interest in any romantic complications. Got enough bloody hassle I'm leaving behind here."

"Hmmm, we'll see," the older man says.

Out of all of his siblings, Chris and his father are the most similar in looks. They share the same square build, broad shoulders and slender hips. The same strong jawline and wiry hair, cut short to keep it in check – the only difference being the older man's temples are flecked with silver. Chris has always thought if he looks like his dad in another thirty years, he need not worry.

"And make sure you prioritise seeing the old folks when you arrive," Chris's dad says, his eyes misting over.

"Of course, Dad. I'll give Grandma and Grandpa your love." Chris grips his father's arm. "I know you miss them as much as they miss you."

Chris's father smiles in acknowledgment.

"Right then," Chris continues. "I'd best get going. Don't want to miss my flight."

"Enjoy your European adventure," Chris's father says, pulling his son into a bear-hug.

"I will," Chris replies before disappearing through the airport's revolving doors.

Twenty hours and three flights later, Chris is sitting outside his favourite beach hut. A beer in hand, watching the sun split the sky as it throws out its final throngs of light before slipping below the horizon, making way for the stars. He gazes up towards the heavens and drinks in the tranquillity. This trip already feels different from all his other adventures. They were just holidays or interludes from his normal life in New Zealand. An opportunity to explore some hidden beach or island paradise somewhere in Asia or the South Pacific.

Until now, he's always felt attached to Aotearoa with an unbreakable bungee cord, as if no matter how far he travelled he would always rebound back home. But right now, as he sits on the beach, listening to the sound of the gentle waves breaking onto the shore, something crackles in the surrounding ether. He can't quite put his finger on it, but he can almost taste it in the air. Something has shifted in the universe.

Rather than leaving something behind, he feels as if he's moving towards something. Perhaps it is the anticipation of seeing so many members of his UK family, or reconnecting with his sisters – but he thinks not. This is something he's never felt before. And it's coming. Something exciting. Something or *someone* that is going to change his life forever. Whatever it is, he has no idea, but he feels it fizz in his gut. It doesn't scare him, rather he welcomes it as he allows the feeling to wash over him.

While he sits on the steps of his beach cabin, the cool sand seeping between his toes, he looks out over the flat horizon, the moon rippling on the surface of the water, and surrenders to the sense of this different awareness within him. Whatever it means, or wherever it leads – he knows he will trust it and follow it willingly.

Dear Reader,

Thank you for taking the time to read one of my books – it means a lot!

If you've enjoyed reading the prequel to *The Three Great Loves of Victoria Turnbull* series, then I'm unashamedly asking for your help. I don't have the weight of a massive publishing house behind me to help get the series out there, and the best way for me to reach more readers is via your support.

One of the most powerful things you can do is leave a review on Amazon and/or Goodreads. It doesn't have to be long, just a single sentence will let others know what you thought. Do not underestimate the influence your review can have on a book's success.

- Leave a review on Amazon.com
- Leave a review on Amazon.co.uk
- Leave a review on Goodreads

Or go to your local Amazon store and click the link to leave a review. If you're feeling super generous, please recommend my books to all your friends and your book club (if you have one). Did you know you can invite me to Zoom into your Book Club by emailing me on **hello@isabellawiles.com**

Needless to say, Victoria's (and Chris's story) will begin to unfold in the next instalment ***A Flame Unburned,*** the first full-length novel of the series.

Read on, for a sneaky taster…

A Flame Unburned - Preview

Victoria, New Zealand, December 2007

Dressed head to toe in damask silk with my handsome groom waiting for me at the end of the rose petal-covered aisle, I glance around the smiling faces of our friends and family, many of whom have travelled from all four corners of the globe to be here today. I wish I could reach back in time and tell my younger self everything was, and is, as it should be.

In the darkest moments of my deepest despair, it would have been comforting to know that thirteen years later I would be happier than I could have ever imagined and it would all be worth it.

Every pain. Every heartache.

But back then I wasn't ready. I wasn't capable of loving in this way. I needed to live every twist and turn, experience every high and low. Lose myself in unmitigated passion and unrivalled grief, all on my pre-ordained path to finding true love and inner peace.

How else can I explain the multiple wrong turns and painful mistakes I've made along the way? Looking back it was obvious, really. Right from the very beginning.

When you strip everything away, isn't every child born with two simple needs? To love, and to be loved. I may have encased my adult self in a hard protective shell, hoping it would make me immune to such primal demands, but — *I am that child.*

Just like the babe I'm cradling in my arms as I walk down the aisle and marry my soulmate. Finally, I'm no longer alone.

I have loved and lost, multiple times, but waiting for me at the end of this short walk is the man I was destined to be with all along. Even if it took me over a decade and three 'great loves' to become the person capable of giving and receiving love in this way.

Three different men.

Three different relationships.

Each teaching me something about myself. Each enabling me to grow and transcend. Each shaping me into the woman I am today.

Gazing out over the horizon at the glinting ripples on the surface of the water that lies beyond the beautiful garden in which I'm about to be wed, I squeeze away the tears of joy from the corner of my eyes and inhale sharply as my heart bursts open.

My precious, *precious* heart, which over the years has given so much, trusted so much, and always remained open and vulnerable, even after she'd been stomped on and broken. Maybe deep down *she* always had faith that this day would finally come, and *she* knows that the man standing next to me now will never hurt me. He will forever hold my heart in his and keep me safe — today, tomorrow, always.

I have everything I could ever want and everything I never knew I needed, and looking back, I wouldn't change a thing. Not one bit of it.

Not the heartache.

Not the betrayals.

Not the passion, nor the pain.

I would do it all again if I knew it would lead me right back here, to this exact moment.

Thirteen years ago, I had no way of knowing the journey I was destined to take, but it all started the year Chris came into my life...

Order your copy of A Flame Unburned here

A Flame Unburned

A HIDDEN SECRET, AN UNFORGIVABLE BETRAYAL, ONE ALL-CONSUMING PASSION.

'Fast-paced, character-rich and emotionally charged, this book has it all. A sheer joy to read. You won't want it to end.' – **Imogen Clark. Million copy bestselling author of Where the Story Starts.**

Victoria Turnbull has a job she loves, shares a house with her best friend, and her posh boyfriend loves her. On paper her life is perfect, but in reality she's lost and floundering, until a trip to the ballet gives her a glimpse of what is missing.

When Christopher Williams, the carefree back-packing Kiwi, lands unexpectedly in her life and seduces her, believing it's fate—she falls hard. And so begins their tempestuous relationship.

However, Vicky is soon trapped by a hideous secret, and when Chris's passion for her is matched by an equally hot-headed temper—she's forced to make unimaginable sacrifices.

Can Vicky forgive her past, before dark truths unravel and destroy her future? Or can Chris overcome his demons before he drives Vicky away?

Set in the early 1990s and twisting and turning around the globe, from the historic **English Countryside** to the breathtaking vistas of **New**

Zealand; via the scorching hot sun of the **Greek Islands**, the contradictions of **Hong Kong** and the furore of **London**, this fearless coming-of-age love story—the first in *The Three Great Loves of Victoria Turnbull* trilogy from new writer Isabella Wiles—is a story about discovering the most important love of all. The love for one's self—despite your flaws.

A perfect read for fans of Jodi Picoult, Elizabeth Gilbert & Colleen Hoover's 'It Ends With Us'.

Readers love *A Flame Unburned:*

'A gloriously heart-rending, compelling and twisty pleasure.' **Amazon Reviewer**

'Wonderfully written. I could not put it down. It's rather unusual today to encounter a novel like this and all the more remarkably by a new author.' **Hidden Gems**

'A tumultuous love story and a compelling read. Isabella Wiles is a modern-day Sidney Sheldon or Judith Krantz – epic novels, intercontinental, spanning years.' **Hidden Gems**

'The storytelling is most lyrical and the descriptions of the various settings so enchanting.' **Chick Lit Club**

'Make sure you have a hanky handy because the roller coaster ride will have you in tears at one point or another. Great book. I can't wait for the next one to see where this goes from here.' **Amazon Reviewer**

Order your copy now

About the Author

By day, Isabella Wiles is the CEO of her own Management Consultancy, something she loves but considers both a blessing and a curse. A curse because it takes her away from home, but a blessing because by night, whilst waiting for endless planes in faceless airports, or while stuck on trains with rubbish Wi-Fi, it allows her the opportunity to indulge her secret passion—writing compelling women's book club fiction.

She has written hundreds of business articles, reviews, and multiple bestselling works of non-fiction under the name Nicola Cook, which are published internationally and translated into multiple languages, however *The Three Great Loves of Victoria Turnbull* series is her first foray into writing fiction.

The bare bones of what has since become this prequel novella was initially included in the original version of *A Flame Unburned* when it was first published in 2018 under the title *Belonging*.

With the support of a new editor and following a complete overhaul of her initial work she re-released a re-edited edition of her debut novel in 2021 under the new title *A Flame Unburned* together with this fully fleshed origin story as this prequel novella *A Life Unstarted*. The final two books in the series, *A Promise Unmade* and *A Star Unborn* followed shortly after.

When she is not sitting on trains or stuck in airports (or because she's spent much of 2020 at home like the rest of the world!) she lives in the north-east of England with her long-suffering husband, their two children and one looney Bassett Hound named Connie.

Acknowledgments

Wow! What a twelve months it's been. Who could have predicted the way 2020, and the first few months of 2021, would unfold for us all. The worldwide pandemic touched everyone and I hope that wherever you were, and whomever you were with, you were able to keep your chin up and do the best you could, as we all muddled through. Hopefully reading books during that time, helped keep you sane. Writing them sure as hell helped me!

Without the never-ending support of my amazing husband sharing the burden of home-schooling, shopping for vulnerable family members and keeping everyone's spirits up whilst we adapted to our new-normal, this manuscript would never have made it through the edits. It's been a crazy and intense twelve months and I'm forever grateful to have you by my side, my darling.

I'm indebted to my select team of ALPHA readers, Kate Freeman, Sarah Miller and Bianca Robinson – you're becoming quite the crack crew and I trust your instincts implicitly. Please keep giving me your unfiltered and honest feedback. Every note helps shape the story into a better read for everyone else. And to all my wider BETA readers and supporters—I'm so very grateful for all your encouragement and kind words as I share the 'almost finished' drafts with you all.

Without the support of the Salts Mill gang of fellow authors

Imogen Clark, Meg Cowley, Debbie Ioanna and Holly Lyne, I would have gone doo-lally this past year. I'm massively grateful for all your 'virtual' support ladies. I look forward to the day when we can meet again for tea, cake and a good 'ole chin wag about all things bookish. I know I can always turn to you when I'm having a crisis of confidence or need help with a random technical question. Thank you for all the pick-me-ups, suitably peppered with random cat videos, or in Imogen's case—lots of pictures of sheep!

Huge thanks also to Zoë Markham from Markham Correct for her exceptional copy editing skills. Never again shall I attempt to 'turn down the corner of my eyes' — I'm still giggling about that one. Your input has helped elevate my work further and I look forward to our continued partnership.

Writing the backstory to Victoria's character allowed me the opportunity to reminisce about my own trip to Istanbul in the 1990s and to draw on some fond memories with my dear friend Antonia Maynard. Although our trip didn't turn out anything like Victoria and Mel's, it was fun to reminisce about our time there. Love you, Tun.

And finally, thank you to you—my reader. I'm always humbled, knowing that you have chosen to read my stories. Your encouragement inspires me to push myself to always serve up my very best work. Please do share your comments and feedback on my Facebook Page, follow me on Instagram and ensure you sign up to my newsletter at www.isabellawiles.com to get on the list about new releases.

Through my writing, I relish tackling challenging (and often taboo) themes, but trust that by setting my stories against emotive backdrops and threading them with love, passion and most importantly—hope, they also leave you feeling uplifted and thoroughly satisfied. However, if you (or someone you know) has been the victim of a sexual assault, and my writing has stirred up some strong emotions, then I've included some contact details of organisations that can help.

Thank you everyone. Right, it's time for me to go and do it all again.

Much love,

Izzy x

This is a work of fiction. Names, characters, places, events and incidents are either products of the author's imagination or used fictitiously. Any resemblance to actual persons, living or dead, or actual events is purely coincidental.

ISBN E-Book: 978-1-9996529-3-7
ISBN Paperback: 978-1-9996529-6-8
ISBN Large Print Paperback: 978-1-9996529-7-5

Published by Aurora Independent Publishing.

A Life Unstarted is written in British English.
Cover design: BooksCovered
Edited by: Markham Correct

Resources

If you are a victim of domestic violence or sexual abuse – or know someone who needs support – below are a list of organisations in the UK who can help.

Refuge National Domestic Abuse Helpline
www.nationaldahelpline.org.uk
Tel: 0808 2000 247

Women's Aid
www.womensaid.org.uk

Samaritans
www.samaritans.org
Tel: 116 123

Printed in Great Britain
by Amazon

18018419R00079